THE

C000001908

SMART

CONNECTOR

THE ENTREPRENEUR'S BLUEPRINT FOR BUSINESS RELATIONSHIP SUCCESS

Why connecting smartly builds your influence, wealth and success as an entrepreneur

Reader endorsements

"An unmissable read from this talented and insightful business author. This is a well thought out and crafted piece of work that every ambitious entrepreneur needs to read."   **Cameron Noble**

"This book will change the way you approach your business enabling you to focus on what really matters – growing and scaling through people. It has revolutionised my approach to both my business and personal relationships. Highly recommended."

Mark Pearson

"Jane's clear and articulate debate on the importance of influence and connection has provided me with a fantastic road map for people success. I will definitely be implementing her strategies in my own business." **Andy Arter**

"Jane's well thought out, written and researched book is a delight. It's entertaining, easy to read and full of valuable insights to improve my business and relationships."   **Matthew White**

The "Smart Connector" has helped me understand why the most successful and respected entrepreneurs in the world put people first."   **Lisa Daly**

"This book is a powerful roadmap for anyone who wishes to improve their leadership and interpersonal skills. It should be required reading for every business leader."   **Cindy Cheng**

"This book was hard to put down once I started reading it, I was truly impressed with how much research and thought has been put into the concepts of cultivating true and honest business relationships." **Brian Smithies**

THE
SMART
CONNECTOR

THE ENTREPRENEUR'S BLUEPRINT FOR BUSINESS RELATIONSHIP SUCCESS

Why connecting smartly builds your influence, wealth and success as an entrepreneur

JANE
bayler

jane@janebayler.com

Published by Jane Bayler

Copyright 2019 by Jane Bayler

The right of Jane Bayler to be identified as the author of this work has been
asserted by her in accordance with the Copyright, Designs and Patents Act
1988.

All rights reserved. No part of this publication may be reproduced, stored in a
retrieval system, or transmitted in any form or by any means without the prior
written permission of the author and publisher except in accordance with the
provisions of the Copyright, Designs and Patents Act 1988.

ISBN: 9781086326000

This book is dedicated to my three beautiful girls,
Immy, Lauren, and Jess,
who inspire me to be the very best version of myself, always.

Table of Contents

PREFACE

"The real competitive advantage in any business is one word only, which is 'people'."

Sheryl Sandberg, COO of Facebook
and Founder of Leanin.org

"I am part of the whole, all of which is governed by nature. I am intimately related to all of the parts which are of the same kind as myself. If I remember these two things I cannot be discontented with anything that arises out of the whole, because I am connected to the whole."

Marcus Aurelius (121–180 AD)
Philosopher and Roman Emperor

"We are hardwired to connect with others. It's what gives purpose and meaning to our lives, and without it there is suffering."

Brene Brown, Author and Researcher

"You can succeed best and quickest by helping others to succeed."

Napoleon Hill, Author of Think and Grow Rich

"Whatever affects one directly, affects all indirectly."

Martin Luther King Jr., Social Activist and Minister

"Stay away from negative people. They have a problem for every solution."   Albert Einstein, Physicist and Inventor

"It's possible for ordinary people to choose to be extraordinary."
Elon Musk, Co-founder and CEO, Tesla,
Co-founder, PayPal, SpaceX, and the Boring Company

"Stop thinking about business in terms of your selfish desires, whether it's money, dreams or 'do what you love.' Instead, chase needs, problems, pain points, service deficiencies, and emotions."
MJ DeMarco, Author and Entrepreneur

"It's amazing what you can accomplish if you don't care who gets the credit."
Harry S. Truman, US President, 1945 to 1945

"If people like you, they'll listen to you. But if they trust you, they'll do business with you."
Zig Ziglar, Entrepreneur and Motivational Speaker

"Spread love everywhere you go. Let no one ever come to you without leaving happier."
Mother Teresa, Missionary and
Nobel Peace Prize winner

"You can't change how people treat you or what they say about you. All you can do is change how you react to it."
Mahatma Gandhi, Politician and Social Activist

"A company's culture is the foundation for future innovation. An entrepreneur's job is to build the foundation."
Simon Sinek, Author and Marketing Consultant

"Surround yourself only with people who are going to take you higher."   Oprah Winfrey, Media Mogul

"People rarely remember what you said, but they do remember whether you genuinely listened to them."

Greg Baer, Founder and CEO of Real Love

"If you want to go fast, go alone. If you want to go far, go together."

Ancient African proverb

"You can get the same airplanes. You can get the same ticket counters. You can get the same computers. But the hardest thing for a competitor to match is your culture and the spirit of your people."

Herb Kelleher, Southwest Airlines CEO

"No man is an island, entire of itself; every man is a piece of the continent, a part of the main. Any man's death diminishes me, because I am involved in mankind, and therefore never send to know for whom the bells tolls; it tolls for thee."

John Donne, Poet (1572–1631)

"Imperfection is beauty, madness is genius and it's better to be absolutely ridiculous than absolutely boring."

Marilyn Monroe, actress

"Try not to become a person of success, but rather try to become a person of value."

Albert Einstein, Physicist and Inventor

"Always treat your employees exactly as you want them to treat your best customers."

Stephen Covey, Author of
The 7 Habits of Highly Effective People

"Life's most persistent and urgent question is: What are you doing for others?"

Martin Luther King,
Activist and Civil Rights Leader

"I used to think I was the strangest person in the world, but then I thought there are so many people in the world, there must be someone who feels the same way I do. Well, I hope that if you're out there and read this, know that, yes, it's true. I'm here, and I'm just as strange as you."   Frida Kahlo, Artist

"When it comes to human dignity, we can't make compromises."
Angela Merkel, German Chancellor

"Courage is what it takes to stand up and speak. Courage is also what it takes to sit down and listen."
Richard Branson, Entrepreneur

"A good head and a good heart are a formidable combination."
Nelson Mandela, Politician, Activist,
and Nobel Peace Prize Winner

"Live every day as if it were your last, because someday you're going to be right."   Muhammed Ali, Boxer

INTRODUCTION

You've just read a range of inspirational quotes from some of the world's most respected past and present leaders to emphasise that nothing is more important in life than connection.

The quality of your relationships with others dictates the quality of your life, and the quality of your business relationships determines the performance of your business. If you agree with this statement, this book about business relationships and entrepreneurial success is definitely for you.

Each chapter of this book has been thoroughly researched to bring you the best contemporary thinking on entrepreneurship and business relationship success. But it also draws on my personal fifteen-year history as a high-level executive in the tough international environment of media in London, and my subsequent entrepreneurial journey, as I hope to give you the opportunity to learn from my personal experience too.

An attitude of giving is at the heart of connection, both in business and life. Too many entrepreneurs don't understand this. They approach their business and personal relationships from a perspective of take. Their behaviour betrays their mindset, and they're always more transparent than they realise. They're so trapped in their own unfulfilled needs that they remain blind to the needs of others. As a result, their interactions become limited, dull, and focussed entirely on 'what's in it for me?' They never just hang out to have fun, make someone else smile, laugh, or feel great about themselves. This is the successful, long-game approach for ambitious entrepreneurs and leaders. Life's so much more fun, and business more profitable, when you adopt the Smart Connector way. These are the attitudes and behaviours that make others feel great about their choice to engage with you.

One of the most successful entrepreneurs in the world, Richard Branson, who according to a Forbes estimate is worth $4.9 billion, said, "Success in business is all about people, people, people", and "It's amazing what doors can open if you reach out to people with a smile, a friendly attitude, and a desire to make a positive impact." He also said, "Master the art of communication, and a new world opens, where you can influence and inspire others more successfully than you ever imagined." He's someone all entrepreneurs look up to, and if he's saying people are the key to success, who are we to argue?

All successful leaders have the ability to put themselves in another person's shoes. They're interested in others as individuals, rather than seeing them as their job functions, or as opportunities they can leverage. They constantly ask themselves how they can create value for the people they serve. They're not hung up on status or the prize they feel they deserve for their efforts. They just scatter goodwill like colourful jewels wherever they go. Such people are the natural influencers of our world. They draw others toward them and inspire loyalty and respect. I've seen many times over how, for people like this, fantastic opportunities open up constantly. This is the Smart Connector way, and it can be your way too. All it takes is knowledge and the willingness to try.

Becoming a people person goes further than this. In every business relationship, there's a junction, or fork in the road, where character and integrity are put to the test. This is the point where someone's true people skills really emerge. Many entrepreneurs prioritise profit over people, but this is not the route to long-term success. Indeed, it's been proven that this is actually bad for business. Businesses only prosper when they innovate, create and deliver value, which are qualities that only people can deliver. Not those who come to work to perform tasks, but those who are genuinely inspired by the mission of the business they serve.

It's good for your business, as well as your personal life, to engage with others in a forgiving and compassionate way. In the event of conflict, always compromise to achieve mutual value. Do everything within your power to resolve your people problems, both inside and outside your business environment. People come first, always.

I want you to get massive value from The Smart Connector. Whether you dip into it occasionally or read it from cover to cover, I'm sure you'll find plenty in it that is helpful and applicable to your own business or life. If you'd like to chat with me personally to discuss any of the topics I cover and receive input on your own business or relationships, please get in touch at: jane@janebayler.com. I'd love to hear from you!

A deeply personal story

Before you dive in, and with your permission, I'd like to share a deeply personal story with you. My success in business was underpinned by some tough personal challenges. I grew up in a family that was overwhelmed by my mother's addiction and mental illness, so I spent much of my childhood trying to escape from my crazy and chaotic home life. The value I place on relationships was initially fuelled by observing the disconnection and isolation of my parents' lives, and vowing with my heart and soul that I would live differently myself. I also realised earlier than most that I had no one to watch my back, which drove my ambition and achievements. But it was later on, and after several painful and humbling lessons, that I joined the dots, and realised that suffering does not have to accompany success. No one should settle for second best when it comes to relationships.

ACOAs (adult children of alcoholics) have specific characteristics that draw us personally, as adults, toward people who are more likely to hurt rather than help us. We tend to either become alcoholics ourselves, like my brother, who sadly died at the age of forty-nine, we marry them, or we find other compulsive personalities to fulfil our abandonment needs. That was certainly my story. I let some toxic and exploitative people into my life, and often felt I had little choice but to accept their behaviour and the value they placed on me. Today, and as a result of the lessons I've learned in life and business, I'm so clear on the standards I expect from others, and so relaxed about communicating them, that I attract only the best and most ethical people to me. As a result of this, every relationship I enter into contributes immediately to both my success and happiness. And if it doesn't, I just exit promptly and peacefully. I wish I'd been able to read my own book all those years ago, as it would have saved me so much heartache and pain!

It's important to understand that business relationships mirror life. If you become a better people person in business, the same thinking and skills show up in your personal life. This results in you becoming the very best and most empowered version of yourself throughout every day and in every situation.

More about my career history: driven by my desire to escape the troubles of my family, I did well academically and left home at the age of seventeen. I attended Goldsmith's College in London, and after gaining a (commercially worthless) degree in English Literature and Drama, I was ill-equipped for the challenge of carving out a career in the expensive city of London. So, like many other entrepreneurially inclined Goldsmith's alumni such as Julian Clary, Vic Reeves, Damon Albarn, Damian Hirst, Vivienne Westwood, and Malcolm McLaren (I was in good company, ha-ha), I just rolled up my sleeves and got on with it.

I started my career as a freelance assistant art director and set designer in film and television. I didn't understand the formal concept of networking at that time, but had noticed that hanging around in the right places, with the right people, led to opportunities. So that's what I did. I worked on several amazing projects as a result, and with so many talented people, who I am still grateful today to have had the privilege to connect with.

Looking back, I realise that people often kept me around because I made them feel good, not because I was a valuable design talent who made their work easier. This was a notoriously competitive industry, in which many who were better qualified and more naturally gifted failed to gain a foothold. I saw that people achieved success through their ability to build and maintain relationships with others as well as their innate talent. It was, as it is in every business sector, all about people.

After three years of working non-stop on some exciting and demanding creative projects, I became interested in the business side of media and television and became employed instead. I moved into the corporate world and rose through the ranks, managing key accounts and developing business for television companies and for the global advertising group Young and Rubicam. I was then approached by the owner of an international design company who asked me to be his MD. I grew the profits of his company, and helped him sell it. By this time, I was a single parent and this was an opportunity for me to quit work (after the sale) and start a business from home. The business was sold within three years to US communications group Interpublic. This gave me a payout of several hundred thousand pounds, which enabled me to exit my high-level corporate career and spend time raising my three girls when they were small. I was so relieved to get out of this lonely, high-pressure environment. And hugely grateful to have had the opportunity to "cash in" when I did, giving me the chance to properly parent my children, and provide them with the love and stability I'd never had.

The higher I'd climbed in my corporate career, and the more I earned, the sadder I'd felt. Like a performing seal, I'd only ever been trained for others. My training was designed to make others very rich. So, I was excited not just to have more time for my girls, but also to combine it with the challenge of entrepreneurship, by building a small business that I could monetise for myself.

Nothing prepared me for the reality of my exit from the corporate world. Although I was happy to be able to spend time with my children, I struggled with the loss of status and the mundane reality of rearing young children, as well as being married to a man whose rage and unpredictable mood swings (it turned out) were almost as bad as the ex I'd left a few years before. I built up a successful children's group tuition business, which brought in cash flow and enabled me to combine looking after my children with earning a living. But behind closed doors, I was still suffering. Despite the joy I felt in my children, I felt sad and lonely so much of the time. Now I know that as a result of my early experiences, I was blind to the warning signs of people who were going to be bad for me, and I confused love with control. No one had taught me the standards I should set for myself in relationships, or warned me of the impact my people choices would have on my wellbeing. I won't make the same mistake again, and I hope this book will help you not to either. Because business is personal and personal is business. The two, in my view, are inextricably linked.

It was a huge shock when I was diagnosed with my breast cancer in 2011. My family had a terrible history with this disease, with both my grandmothers, as well as my aunt, having died young from it. My youngest daughter was only eight when I was diagnosed, and my greatest fear was that I was going to die too and leave her, as well as my older girls, motherless. I had it bad, I was told, with eleven out of twelve lymph nodes affected and a large tumour that was attached to my chest wall. I had chemotherapy, radiotherapy, six major operations, and ten years of adjuvant hormone treatment. But helped by advances in conventional and alternative medicine, as well as the expert care and attention I received from all the medical professionals who treated me, I'm alive and well today. I'm so grateful to all the wonderful people who showed me the strength and power of unconditional love and care.

The worst time of all during my treatment came at the very end of my chemotherapy. I attended hospital for my last dose, which, as the result of an extravasation injury, ended up flooding the tissues of my arm from hand to shoulder. This caused a skin-blistering, irreversibly vein-collapsing, second-degree chemical burn that left me in agony for weeks. Coming back from this experience, my priorities had changed for good. I'd become a different person—someone more inclined to live for the moment and take bigger and bolder risks with my life. I'd also become unwilling to settle for anything other than the life I truly wanted, which meant I became more demanding and less accommodating towards others. This contributed to my husband having an affair and leaving me, which, thankfully, made the resolution of our painful marriage very simple.

The cancer "experience" had positive outcomes in unexpected ways, but most valuable of all, it gave me the gratitude and appreciation that I bring to each and every day.

My career in property, which I picked up a few years ago, was defined from the start by my desire to build wealth and profitable partnerships with others. I've had some truly amazing wins (as this is an industry where success is rewarded handsomely) and made some powerful friendships, but I also had more painful lessons to learn about people and their integrity. Sadly, and like far too many others that enter this industry with funds to invest, I became entangled at the start of my journey with some unethical and inexperienced people who caused me to lose a significant amount of money. This is a complex story for another day and for my live training. But stay posted, as I will be revealing EVERYTHING to you in time, as it is my sincere wish for you to never go through this pain yourself!

If I started on my property journey that would be a whole new book, as property is still one of my favourite topics, and a hobby as well as a business interest of mine. But I'm sticking to the subject of business relationships here, as this book is aimed at all entrepreneurs, regardless of their business sector.

Thank you for taking the time to read about me. I hope you've found my story interesting and that you receive great value from my book.

CHAPTER ONE:
Why People Help You Win in Business

In this chapter, I'm going to look at why people skills matter so much in business. And I'm going to give you five 'principles of influence' to improve both your business and personal outcomes with others. The reason this is important is because no matter how many qualifications or skills you have, or how many prestigious companies or clients you've worked with or for, there's only one thing that will make you stand out from your competition. And that's how you deal with people.

How engagement builds success

Many entrepreneurs rely on qualities such as energy, charisma, passion and drive to get what they want in life. They're like business party starters. They get things moving. Their positive energy is infectious. People love to get into their slipstream, so it's easy for them to get a business going and attract people to it. But however delightful it is to be around these inspiring types, energy, enthusiasm and passion aren't enough to build lasting engagement. Energy, enthusiasm and passion create a parallel expectation of strong leadership. And when leaders can't deliver on this expectation, their followers can become disillusioned and turn against them. This results in employee churn, boardroom or business partner battles, defecting or disloyal suppliers, and low-engagement, price-driven customers. In other words, massive headaches and problems! And who wants that when there's a better way to deal with their business and life?

You can't fast track connection

Today's business landscape is powered by technology, which generates ways to do everything faster, as well as more efficiently and cheaply. Innovation and cost savings are wonderful for business, but you can't fast track or cheapen human connection in the same way. Email and texts have pushed the boundaries of relationships in terms of how much and how often we "touch" someone as opposed to how much time we spend with them. They're efficient ways to communicate and get things done. But human connection doesn't evolve through these channels. Trust and engagement are only built through the face-to-face or personal time we invest with others. So, the best investment you can make in your business and your future is to invest time with your key people, instil them with your values, and inspire them to build powerful relationships with others in turn. It is people who make, buy, deliver, sell and consume your products and services. When you invest in people, you're investing in your own success. It's as simple as that.

If you're an entrepreneur, take time to invest in the junior people in your business as well as your directors, suppliers and customers. They'll be so appreciative of your attention and efforts that it will make them great ambassadors for you. You don't have to give them the same focus or attention as your higher level connections, but a few kind words and expressions of interest will go a long way to ensuring their loyalty and dedication to your business.

Why great leaders put people first

Some entrepreneurs have a strong technical- or skill-based orientation and believe, as a result, that the solution to dealing with people is to systemise, buy in or delegate the "people stuff". If that's a mindset you subscribe to, improving your people skills is even more critical for you. If you don't know how to lead yourself and others, your vision and values will be hijacked and power plays will start happening all around you. It's easy for people who are technically brilliant to bury themselves in their work—but if this is the life you want, it may be better for you to work as a freelancer instead. If you're technically brilliant and running a business, you'll need to make your relationships great too. There's no getting away from the challenge!

Customers are at the heart of every business. Satisfying customers profitably is the key to success. Bring your very best customers and team members into your inner circle, where you build loyalty and engagement through face-to-face and personal interaction. Customers will buy from you if you have a great product, but your competitors are constantly innovating, so you can't rely on your product alone to sustain sales. You will only truly satisfy your customer and build their loyalty and engagement if you are meeting their constantly shifting needs. If you have tens, hundreds, thousands or even millions of subscribers or customers, you won't be able to communicate with them individually, but you can still engage with them powerfully, communicate with them constantly, and put feedback loops in place that gives their voice the opportunity to be heard. Taking your lead from massively successful influencers like Oprah, Tony Robbins and Richard Branson, every entrepreneur should also aim to build an engaging personal brand and provide daily inspiration and value to those they serve.

It's so important to develop the high-level habits of leadership if you want to achieve success through people. You'll need to fine-tune your intuition, emotional intelligence and know when and how to let your emotions guide you. You'll need to communicate promptly and clearly, particularly when challenging issues arise. A true people person lets others win—in fact, helps them win—and never looks to exploit or gain advantage at someone else's expense. This isn't just fluffy talk. Research has consistently shown that businesses that build authentic, honest, open, and collaborative relationships with their customers, partners, team and suppliers are significantly more profitable (and sustainably profitable) than companies that treat these same people deceptively, antagonistically and manipulatively. Great people skills always win. It's to do with trust. Once people get beyond the survival stage of their careers to the point where they can choose who they work with, they give their loyalty and commitment to those they trust. It's human nature.

The five principles of business influence

Here are my top five principles of business influence to help you build trust and meaningful connections with others:

1. **Empathy**. This is emotional intelligence—the ability to relate to people as individuals and see a situation from their perspective as well as your own. People need to feel heard and seen by you before they'll accept your influence, and empathy is the magic sauce that helps with this. Empathy is distinct from sympathy or advice, which are "outside in" behaviours. Empathy makes people feel understood because it helps you connect with them through the emotions that underpin their experience. There are techniques that can make you better at this, but they won't be effective unless you're fully in touch with and able to access your own feelings too. So, empathy is helped by a habit of introspective reflection that enables you first to connect with your own feelings and then use them to appreciate the experience of others, without them having to spell things out for you.

2. **Clarity**. Powerful communication only happens when you're clear in your own mind. When you've given up your valuable time to be in the company of others, you need to know why you're there and what outcome you desire. And if the other person has a different agenda, use the time you spend with them to get clear about this before you move on to anything else. Clarity helps you quickly resolve conflicts of interest or values, but only if you're able to spot them and bold enough to address them. Clarity starts with you knowing your personal reason why and your business reason why. It's underpinned by your values, your goals and your objectives. Leaders need to do the work to identify these so they can be clear and consistent in their dealings with others.

3. **Patience**. Be calm and patient if you're raising a difficult issue or trying to strike a deal with others. This keeps you in control and ensures the other person will be more open to a solution. Patience is linked to our ability to embrace ambivalence or uncertainty, which can feel uncomfortable at

first. Pushing someone too aggressively, or issuing unreasonable ultimatums, is an act of dominance, which everyone dislikes. Whilst you should always be decisive, a lack of patience is perceived as a red flag to many in business. At its worst, impatience can lead to irrational behaviour or temper tantrums. And blowing your top is the ultimate leadership and communications fail. It destroys trust, sometimes permanently, and always makes tricky situations worse.

4. **Listening.** Active listening requires you to step outside yourself and focus wholeheartedly on another for as long as it takes to truly appreciate their perspective. It helps in two ways: it tells the person that you're genuinely invested in the relationship, and it helps you get a clearer understanding of their values. Active listening takes conscious effort and requires you to listen a lot more than you talk—probably in an 80/20 ratio. Like other principles of influence, this is a developable skill. Active listening is a fully engaged conversation. It involves letting someone talk until they've finished speaking and pausing to think about your answer before you respond. You'll need to make sounds that indicate attentiveness, as well as give feedback in the form of a paraphrased rendition of what they have said. Active listening is the best form of information gathering there is. It breaks down assumptions and misinformation to give you true people intelligence.

5. **Trust.** What does it take for you to trust people? And how do you react to a betrayal of trust? Trust is a key issue in business as well as life. You'll need to stop controlling and start trusting people if you want to get the best out of them. But you'll also need to deal with breaches of trust quickly and firmly. Be bold and resist your people-pleasing tendencies. Expect the truth from others and be truthful in return. Remember what you don't say is also a form of lying. If you're one of those people who thinks, "If I haven't admitted to it, I'm not lying", you lack integrity. Tony Robbins says integrity is "Doing what's hard when no one's looking." I would add to this and suggest that it's also "saying what's hard when it won't be received well." To

build the high-level relationships you need, the relationships that will take your business and life to its best level yet, you need to be perceived as trustworthy.

These are the reasons why your people skills are so connected to your business success. In the following chapters, my promise to you is that I am going to help you improve and develop yours so that you become the best leader of both your life and your business.

CHAPTER TWO:
Set and Achieve Your People Goals

It's common for others to enter and exit our lives in ways we don't like—whether it's being hurt in love, falling out with a friend, or something to do with business, such as losing money or being cheated out of something we feel should have been ours. It's also common for us to react to disappointments like these by shutting down and becoming cynical and suspicious. But this attitude will isolate us and make us unhappy. It's also bad for business. We must stay connected to others simply because it is a better and more fulfilling way to live. In business as well as life, we need to be bold with our actions, acknowledge the strength and wisdom we gain from every experience, and use it to make better choices in future. So even if we've been hurt or let down, and even when our actions are going to hurt or disappoint others, we should never shy away from speaking up and asking others to support us in our goals.

You can only "change" yourself

To set and achieve your people goals, it is important to stop trying to control what others are doing and start looking at yourself instead. When we struggle with others, it often comes from us and our faulty patterns of thinking and behaviour. We will always get negative, unhelpful and distracting thoughts. We can't do anything about that—it's our human experience. But these thoughts will pass on their own if we don't add fuel to them by mistaking them for the "truth". If you're unhappy with someone and want them to change, it's important to speak up quickly. Otherwise, resentment will take hold and fester, and this is the fastest way to destroy any relationship.

Tell the other person directly and specifically what's upsetting you, then tell them the change you're looking for. Be open to them challenging you or correcting your assumptions, as you're not always going to interpret things correctly. If they accept the change you're asking them to make, agree on a timeline and clear consequences for any inaction, which passes the freedom of choice to them. If they reject your request and challenge you, decide whether there is something you have learned about yourself from your interaction and thank them if this is the case. Then, release them to get on with their life and go back to enjoying yours.

Not everyone is comfortable with this super direct style of interaction, but in business, this is what builds respect and gets results. And in life, it gives you the peace and freedom to be with people who love and accept the real, imperfect you, rather than some dull, "nice" version that no one believes in. When you hold on to your feelings and don't express them, you come across as weak. People respect others who are emotionally authentic and willing to risk imperfect engagement.

Audit your relationships

As an entrepreneur, it's important to put aside time to work ON your business as well as IN it. Make time to reflect on your overall strategy, as well as review the performance of your partners and team. Do this when you're blocking off time to do what the renowned leadership expert Stephen Covey calls "Quadrant Two activities". This involves recognising new opportunities and building new relationships to serve them. Are your existing relationships serving your vision and goals, and if not, what changes do you need to make? Are there new relationships you need to build, or old relationships you need to shed? What are you doing to inspire and motivate the people associated with your life and business? What more can you do?

Many business owners focus purely on profit and put their "people stuff" last. But auditing your team and network at least quarterly means you're taking a leadership position in your business, and this will significantly improve your profits too. As well as the results you're getting from the people around you, consider what you're giving to them in return. Do you understand what truly motivates those who are working for and with you? Are you able to communicate through their values? How do you recognise and reward them for doing great work? Do they have opportunities for recognition, progression and autonomy? Do you understand and communicate through their values? Is there anything you or someone else hasn't confronted someone about? Are there some who are sitting back and taking it easy while others take on too much responsibility? How do you ensure everyone in your team is appropriately rewarded for their contribution? Do you have reporting structures, systems, processes and KPIs in place? And most important of all, do you make it a priority for everyone to have fun and enjoy themselves with you?

If you're aiming to grow and scale your business, it's a good idea to put systems in place to leverage or outsource low-level tasks. It's common practice these days for entrepreneurs to engage virtual assistants that work in other countries, but always remember they're still part of your team and therefore need managing too. I know of one outsourcer who sets aside time each year to visit the Philippines and meet with his large virtual team. A couple of days are spent reviewing the work and the next day is spent building team spirit and having fun. He claims the effort and expense has definitely paid off for him.

So to sum up: to be successful in business, always remember to take time out for what Stephen Covey calls your Quadrant Two (important but not urgent) activities. And dedicate a big part of this to auditing and improving both your processes and management of people.

Blueprint for people success

I'd like to share with you my four-step plan to help you make great choices about the people you include in your life as well as your business. This plan will help you draw the right people to you and recognise the ones you should avoid. But here's a disclaimer: if you're the wrong person yourself—if you're not at least trying to adopt rigorously ethical behaviours and principles—you're likely to stay stuck with the wrong ones. Remember, like attracts like, so as well as educating yourself on the people you should avoid, you always need to set high standards for your own conduct too.

Step one is to get clear about other people's values and how they fit with yours. If you ask someone what their values are, they'd probably say something like "I'm loyal, honest, and reliable." People generally overestimate their integrity, and it's important to remember that words are cheap. Integrity only shows up in someone's behaviour over a period of time. So, what you can do instead is monitor a person's actions more than their words until you can recognise patterns. Look for congruence. Do they tell the truth about themselves? Do what they said they'd do when they said they'd do it? And humility, which shows up as them admitting their mistakes and flaws rather than blaming others. Look also for people who have a vision for their life that they're willing to share with you and a respectful, win-win attitude. People like this will bring peace and joy to your life and business, instead of them draining it with negativity and conflict.

You're you, and sometimes that won't suit others

Step two is to recognise how and in what ways someone defines fulfilment. If you have a big and ambitious vision that demands sacrifice on your part—for example, if you're focussed on achieving success through entrepreneurship—be on the lookout for saboteurs and dream stealers. No matter how "nice" they are, people who subscribe to average values won't necessarily understand or be able to support you on your journey; in fact, they may try to change you instead. Not everyone has to be on the same path as you, but make sure they at least understand and support the vision you've shared with them. And if they pout, sulk or try to make life difficult for you as a result, don't cave in or pander to them. Stay kind, but firm, and true to you.

It's common for entrepreneurs to have life partners who resent their commitment to work. If that's you, understand that they didn't choose to marry or be with a workaholic. They chose you, and part of their hopes and dreams were spending time with someone who is willing to prioritise them at least some of the time. No matter how busy you are, it is important to make time for the people who love you, as long as they stay respectful of your needs and values too.

Accept rejection

Step three is to accept the hidden blessing of rejection. Every disappointment or rejection creates a fresh opportunity. You should always celebrate a relationship, whether it comes from you or the other person, because someone or something better is just around the corner. Always appreciate and give thanks for the closing of one door and the opening of another. However painful, if a business or personal relationship wasn't meant to be, it was for a good reason— probably because of the misaligned values that I've already referred to. If someone simply doesn't get the bliss of you, move on! Don't waste your attention and interest. Every rejection, however upsetting it seems at the time, frees you up for the chance of a better and more fulfilling future.

Assumptions are not shortcuts

Step four is to lower your assumptions and expectations with someone you don't know well. When you enter into a new relationship, in business or life, it's common for assumptions to go into overdrive and for expectations to skyrocket. Of course, this is mostly followed by disappointment. The more unfamiliar a person is to you, the more you're in the dark about their true nature. They're therefore more prone to surprise you in unwelcome and potentially negative ways. Remember, expectation is based on the false assumption that others share our values, and this is mostly not true. Give yourself time to get to know someone before deciding where they fit in relation to you. Never be hasty, make a premature commitment that would be difficult to reverse, or accept the pushiness of others. In fact, the more pushy someone is the less trustworthy they are likely to be.

So to sum up: your four-step plan for goal setting in relationships is (a) to get clear about someone's integrity, (which only shows up through their actions over time), (b) assess their values and aspirations to see whether they will support or negatively impact yours, (c) stay open to and celebrate your relationship fails, and (d) keep your expectations low until you've got to know someone and have decided whether they're worthy of taking up that important place in your business or life.

CHAPTER THREE:
Inspire and Motivate Others

The power of possibility

Inspiring and motivating others is linked to the different skill sets of leadership and management. Many think it's the job of leaders to inspire and the job of managers to motivate. People with fixed mindsets will have you believe you're either a leader or a manager, and whether you're one or the other depends on your innate personality. They'll also believe you can either inspire or motivate, but you can't do both. The same belief system also says that entrepreneurs are born not made. This thinking is unhelpful for SME entrepreneurs. You can learn to inspire as well as motivate. Just as you can learn to be an entrepreneur. All it takes is an open mind, the humility to learn, and the willingness to take action and put what you've learned into practice. Of course, many leaders prefer to spend their time inspiring, creating and engaging managers to motivate and maintain structure in their business. This is, of course, fine, but whether you have a dedicated manager or not, it's important to believe that with the right support, anything is possible. You can motivate AND lead, even when you find someone to take the tasks you dislike off your plate.

Thinking in absolutes is toxic to your wellbeing. Black and white thinking stifles growth and shuts down meaningful communication. You'll come across this type of thinking all the time in the world of "average", which is the world your employed friends, family, and neighbours inhabit. But as an entrepreneur who is priming yourself for success, I invite you to set yourself apart. Think of yourself as belonging to a parallel universe, one where the power of possibility defines you. Mahatma Gandhi said, "Man becomes what he believes himself to be. If I keep on saying to myself that I can't do a certain thing, I may really become incapable of doing it. On the contrary, if I have the belief that I can, I shall surely acquire the capacity to do it, even if I may not have it at the beginning." With those words in mind, believe that you, too, can be someone who can motivate and inspire. You just have to know how.

How you can inspire

Let's look first at how to inspire. Because of our intrinsic need for growth, all of us are constantly on the lookout for role models to inspire us. Inspiring others, therefore, has a lot to do with behaving like a leader. Whether it's of your business, your family, or simply yourself, every day you have to get up and tell yourself that's what you are. Leaders know who they are and why they do what they do. They have a powerful vision for their lives and businesses and an action plan to fulfil them, which they're able to communicate in a clear and engaging way to others. It's also important for leaders to have integrity because, in order to inspire others, you have to lift them higher and make them think their association with you will help them become better and more fulfilled.

Hold yourself accountable

Without a habit of holding yourself and your actions up to scrutiny, you're probably not the best leader of others. People with strong integrity check in with themselves frequently to reflect on the impact of their actions upon others. They stand up for what they believe in and will only tolerate the same high standards from those around them. If someone behaves badly, they'll react quickly and firmly to make their lack of acceptance clear and will set consequences for the behaviour if repeated. But they'll do this without anger or judgement, as they know no one's perfect. Leaders don't personalise problems (i.e. beat themselves up for something that's outside of their control) or expend energy in a state of blame or negativity. When a difficult issue arises, rather than looking for an external cause, they'll turn the focus back on themselves to ask questions like "How can I be better, stronger, and of more value to prevent this happening again?" or "How can I make my life and business happier and more successful as a result of this new challenge or information?" Leaders hold themselves accountable for their results, and this sets them apart from everyone else.

Stand up for others

True leaders will try never to cause unnecessary harm to anyone, and if they do, they'll be quick to admit what they've done, apologise, and make genuine and lasting amends. They're champions of justice, and if they see someone who's been hurt by another's actions, they'll step in and do what they can to help, even when they risk unpopularity or personal loss. This is because they're aware of their own strength and never hesitate to use it for the benefit of those who are weaker or more vulnerable. I think of leaders like brave lions—demonstrating behaviours that establish their right to be at the top of the food chain.

If you're someone who's used to accepting low standards of behaviour from yourself and others, it can sometimes feel uncomfortable to be up close to someone like this. This is because their approach to life challenges you to be better in turn. This can provoke self-doubt and even some personal guilt, pain or shame. But this is also why so many of us are overwhelmingly drawn to such people. First, because we trust them and feel safe in their presence, and second because becoming the best version of ourselves is something most of us truly aspire to.

The best leaders have been on their own personal and spiritual journey and received guidance from other people or mentors. This is because leadership is not a natural gift—it requires both discipline and self-scrutiny, which is easier to achieve when others are a sounding board.

Communicate through stories

Another important aspect of inspiring others is the ability to communicate through narratives or stories. People love stories and telling them helps others connect emotionally with you. Stories have accompanied our existence for as long as we've been on Earth. They help bypass all the corporate roles, missions, job titles, and functions we hide behind to allow others the bliss of experiencing and connecting with the authentic you. When you're able to communicate through storytelling, you'll naturally inspire others. Of course, some people have a gift in this respect, but really anyone can tell a story as long as they're committed to practising. So, get clear about your dreams and vision. Then practise telling these in story form to others and get them inspired, too.

To recap: to be an effective leader and inspire others, be someone who sets high standards for yourself and others. Act according to a consistently firm but gentle code of behaviour. Then get good at communicating through stories that reveal the authentic you to others.

How you can motivate

Now, let's move on to motivating others, which is more of a management function. Motivating has a lot to do with providing the right conditions and environment for people to flourish. They'll need opportunities for progression, recognition and autonomy, as well as job descriptions they have had some input in and realistically achievable targets.

Four ways you can motivate others are to win trust, earn respect, remain open to possibility and communicate transparently. Like every management practice, this requires discipline and structure. If you're not yet able to hire a full-time manager or team, you'll need to get good at this yourself with some outsourced admin support.

Understand the role of values

A good way to win the trust of others is by showing them that you care and take an interest in them, rather than just viewing them in terms of what they can do for you. Keep it light, as people will only open up to you in accordance with the trust and comfort level you've achieved with them. Rather than behaving in the same way towards everyone, communicate through their individual values; in other words, the things that matter to them.

You can find out people's values by asking them what's most important to them in life. If they say travel, show them ways that their career path can support this passion. If they say family, look at aspects that will help them with this, such as flexible working or an extra holiday allowance for hitting their targets. If they've got children, learn their children's names and ask how they're doing. If they love sport, talk to them about the last game they watched or went to. If they've moved house, ask them what's good about their new area. It all comes back to being sensitive and seeing people as human beings with a need to feel heard and understood, rather than making them feel they only matter because of the job they're doing for you.

Catch people doing well far more than making mistakes and you will win their loyalty, as well as making them feel happier in their work.

Be the real you

A good way to earn respect is simply by being the very best you. A lot of people believe they shouldn't talk about their personal lives to people they meet through work. Either that or because they haven't got a home team or proper support network, they inappropriately reveal all of their darkest and most difficult personal problems to their colleagues, which is often a result of the notoriously tongue-loosening presence of alcohol. This is the fastest way to lose respect and get yourself into situations you'll later regret. So, don't be secretive. Bring the real you to all your dealings with people, but make sure it's the best side of you—the one that is light-hearted, fun and entertaining. Leave the stresses or your more personal problems for your trusted "home team" or a professional to deal with.

Most people particularly respect someone who can demonstrate the ability to face up to and conquer challenges courageously. So, when a problem arises in your business or sector, be transparent about it.

Use the opportunity to either enrol others in finding the solution or tell them what you've done to meet it head-on.

Work harder than others, reward yourself more

People respect those who dedicate themselves wholeheartedly to their business success as well as yours, so if you leave at 5:00 PM and expect others to slave away until 7:30 PM, they won't take it too well. Your respect levels can take a nose dive if others feel you're leaving them with the hard work while you're lazing around on the sofa at home. Always work as hard or harder than the people who work for you, but make sure you reward yourself well for your efforts and the responsibility you carry.

Remaining open to possibility is going back to the issue I mentioned earlier of having a growth rather than a fixed mindset. This means believing in other people's potential to perform. If you're a pessimist who always expects the worst, you'll infect others around you with the same attitude, making them feel miserable and demotivated. Tap into possibility thinking by eliminating your control freak tendencies and giving people a direction, timeline, and, most importantly, the authority to act. Only step in when they struggle or fail. And if they do, review your own expectations as well as their performance, as a blame culture only serves to demotivate and disempower. Take it further if it's your own business by telling people you have zero tolerance for blame. Mistakes should be celebrated and learned from. Reward those who own up to them.

Communicate – the golden rule

Communicating transparently means meeting people's need to know two things: where you stand on any given subject and where they stand with you. When in doubt, overcommunicate. Set yourself a rule that you'll never leave it longer than 24 hours to get back to anyone, since there's nothing more frustrating than not hearing back from someone you've repeatedly tried to get through to. If you're managing people, or you have someone else who is helping you manage them, it's helpful to use performance tools such as KRAs (key results areas), and KPIs (key performance indicators) to give people a sense of direction and safety. Get help (if you're the leader of the business) to set these, and include people's individual goals and aspirations into your planning. Create (or get someone to create for you) a bespoke system of benefits, incentives and career progression, rather than imposing something on them that could be retrofitted onto anyone. Make sure you share positive feedback and good news stories to keep morale high without shying away from the problems or challenges others can help you solve, then watch their respect for your climb.

In summary, to motivate others, communicate clearly and transparently. Don't be a control freak; give others autonomy and the authority to act. Show an interest in their lives and goals. Give them meaningful opportunities for progression and catch them doing well far more than making mistakes. Share your challenges, ideas and good news stories. Take these principles on board and you'll be well on your way to being someone who can both motivate and inspire others.

CHAPTER FOUR:
Understand Your Customer

Never underestimate the importance of customers. These are the people bringing you your bottom-line profit. Without them, you wouldn't have a business at all. Satisfying your customer profitably, therefore, is one of your most important activities as an entrepreneur. If you plan to be in business for a long time, building loyal and sustainable customer relationships give you a massive competitive edge. Many entrepreneurs get too busy working IN their businesses to step back and consider the needs of their customers. Everything they do revolves around themselves and their product, but their front-line staff and customers are treated like commodities. With this approach, your business will struggle. No matter how much effort you put into sales, if you don't take care of your customers once you've acquired them, they won't stick around, and you'll be back to square one.

Happy employees lead to happy customers

Richard Branson often comments on customer excellence, and he is clear that this starts with the way you treat your employees. He said, "Clients do not come first. Employees come first. If you take care of your employees, they will take care of the clients." It makes perfect sense. If your employees are proud to be working for you, if they feel their experience is better and more enjoyable than the one they would have with your competitors, they will feel happy. And happy people tend to treat others well. Of course, you need structure too, but strong leadership and a culture that empowers and appreciates will go a long way towards creating satisfied customers.

Research shows that depending on the industry you're in, acquiring a new customer can be anywhere from 5 to 25 times more expensive than retaining an existing one. It's also proven that increasing customer retention rates by a mere 5% can increase the profit of a business by 25% to as much as 95%. So, if your business is already thriving, it makes sense to put proportionately more of your effort into keeping the customers you've already got than acquiring new ones.

Your evolving customer profile

As your business evolves, your strategy will change and with it your ideal customer profile. It may become a priority to move from a "low-value" customer to a "high-value" one. This has happened to me on a number of occasions as my business changed from the start-up to the growth phase. Depending on the sector your business is in, this may also happen to you. Build a detailed customer profile for each phase of growth. If you're moving on to bigger and better, be very clear about who you're targeting and why. Remember that even if you don't value your existing customers as you once did, neglecting them or treating them as redundant stock can hurt your reputation. So, let your old customers—the ones attached to your start-up phase—go gently, but make sure you service them right up until the last minute and to the best of your ability. If you help them make the transition away from you by recommending one of your competitors who can provide for their needs better than you, they will mostly be really grateful.

How to build customer loyalty

Here are four ways you can understand and meet your customer needs. The first is to communicate with them frequently through multiple touch points. We all love attention, and giving your customers this is a valued compliment, gift and "thank you" that will give you the competitive advantage. Yes, attention can be hard work, but it can also be systemised, giving you a scalable strategy that you only need to revisit every few months or so. Some customers require one-to-one servicing through calls, emails and face-to-face meetings. Others can be serviced through digital communications and feedback loops designed to build trust and solve their problems. Your customers will truly appreciate being able to interact with your business whenever they want, so give them this opportunity. Webinars, podcasts, live streaming and videos are all great ways to generate rapport. Live videos give a more personalised, hands-on experience, and because of their throwaway nature, it's easy to put presentations and product demos in them.

Generating content also helps build referrals because you're constantly "out there" communicating your value. People like to do business with people they're familiar with. The more content you're creating, the more attention you're generating, and the easier it is to build trust amongst your existing customer base. This makes it easier to win and retain new customers, too. If your content allows them to interact with you, it creates the opportunity to understand your customers' pain points, as well as what you can do to overcome them.

Be transparent

The second way to meet your customer needs is to be transparent. There's nothing more infuriating both in personal as well as business relationships than a feeling of not having the full picture or constantly moving goalposts. Let people be clear about your terms of business. Let them know if something changes that affects their experience with you and what you're doing about it. This is being pro-active in your transparency, which is a hallmark of customer service excellence. Answer their questions more fully than they might have anticipated. Overcommunicate and overshare. Treat them as the valuable stakeholder in your business that they are. This will flatter their ego and meet their human need for significance. Of course, you're in charge of what you share with them. They don't need to know everything about your business—especially if it could unnerve or scare them. But they do need to know about the issues that will affect their experience of you, and you should let them tell you what this is rather than you deciding on their behalf.

Offer a great product

The third way to meet your customer needs is to offer a great product. Buyers have more choices than ever, so in most instances, your product or service has to either make your clients money or save them time and money. Study your competitors constantly to see how they do this. Try not to compete on price, as this will eat into your profit, but aim to offer a premium product that people will pay more for. Since the market is always evolving, it is important that your product or service offer is as up to date and relevant as it can be. The only way to ensure this is through market intelligence. So make sure you're at the forefront of changes and developments in your sector.

All businesses need a reason for their customers to buy from them rather than their competitors. This reason is linked to your product or service offer and is called your unique sales proposition (USP). You can discover this by completing the following sentence: Customers buy from me because......

Everyone in your business should understand your USP, as it also sets a benchmark for customer satisfaction and the standard everyone needs to fulfil.

Be enthusiastic

The fourth way to meet your customer needs is to be enthusiastic. People don't just buy what you sell; they also buy you. So how you present yourself has a huge influence on whether they decide to buy from you or not. Emotion is contagious, and if you help your customer tune into positive feelings, they'll always come back for more. The best way to give them this is not through the product itself. It's through your brand and the way you present yourself. Be excited and your customers will get excited too. Be happy and you'll help your customers feel happy too. Tell your story in a way that resonates positively with them and makes them feel they can connect with you.

Always remember that enthusiasm can't be faked. People are intuitive and pick up on signals or vibrations that you're not even aware of. They can feel how much you cherish your business, as well as how dedicated you are to meeting their needs. And once they choose you, they need to experience your continued enthusiasm to serve them. A great way to do this by giving them a quick win—a result that overdelivers, so their confidence in you grows and they, in turn, become more enthusiastic about their choice to work with you.

To achieve powerful customer loyalty, as with every important relationship in your life, you simply need to make it a priority to listen and engage. Overdeliver and overcommunicate is the mantra of customer service success, so always aim to provide massive value. This requires stepping out of your selfish, ego-driven view of the world and placing yourself wholeheartedly in their shoes. Know your customer well enough to both predict their needs and exceed their expectations.

Express gratitude for their decision to work with you and ask them why they chose you instead of others. Find out what's stopping them from going to your competition and ask them if they have ideas for how your products or service could improve. Depending on your business sector, you may have a handful of high-value clients who can answer these questions personally. Or you may have to automate this process through keyword research, focus groups or social listening, which is what people are saying about you online. However you do it, looking after your customers will always reap the best rewards for you.

CHAPTER FIVE:
Why You Must Leverage

The word "leverage" is most commonly used when discussing financial concepts like investment and debt. People who use leverage do it to get a return that is considerably more than the share they put in. Someone who wants to buy a house, for example, will leverage the cash they already have by adding bank funds—in the form of a mortgage—to it. Their available cash may have been enough to buy a small apartment outright, but not the spacious four-bedroom family home in the school catchment area they want for their children. So, they leverage the bank's funds to reach their goal.

The power of social leverage

Many people also leverage their social connections to achieve value in life. Being a natural networker, the social connections I made when my children were young ensured an amazing social life for them. They were invited to endless parties, sleepovers and social events, and even holidays on several occasions. They became the friend of choice for so many, and the reason for this was simply the relationships I invested in with their parents. I also, of course, made sure that value was created in return for them, but on terms that worked for me. For example, because I was very focussed on my children's education, I became known as an expert on educational issues (a personal interest of mine, plus my mother was a teacher so you could say it was in the blood). I would freely give my time to assess other parents' children and advise them on their child's performance and potential, which made them keen to reciprocate in some way. Note this was not connected to any teaching qualification, which I didn't possess. I simply had a passion for education—and I still do.

I would invite other people's children to play with mine, but I would not be the parent, like some, who sat with the children doing arts and crafts. I would make sure they did their homework together, then I'd leverage the other people's children to entertain mine while I paid the bills, tidied up the house, did some work or prepared the evening meal. The social networking I did with other parents also meant I was able to rapidly start a second income stream (a small group tuition business that I ran for my older daughter), ensuring a lucrative source of income for her while she was at university and an extra £1K month cashflow for me that only involved minimal effort for one day each week. When my children were due to sit entrance examinations for the grammar school they all attended, I leveraged the most studious and conscientious children in the class to come to our house and work in a select group alongside mine, which elevated my children's performance and also gave me an income stream (as their parents were happy to pay me for this privilege). Leveraging social connections truly had a massive positive impact on my children, enabling them to fulfil their academic potential and grow up confident, sociable and naturally at ease in the company of others.

Even if you don't have children, social leverage can be an important source of success for you. As I said in my introduction, the social connections I built early in my career ensured an endless stream of exciting work-related opportunities for me. Social connections build goodwill and what's called "social capital", which allows you to leverage the talents, expertise, connections and insights of others. If you're an entrepreneur, building social connections with your team, partners or clients builds all important goodwill that generates huge competitive benefits. People who don't understand the power of social leverage are at a considerable disadvantage in business unless they are natural introverts who have built a systemised, internet-based offer to support their natural character and inclinations, which is also superb leverage!

The power of time leverage

In everyday life, another popular way people use leverage is through their use of time. For example, if you have a child who attends the same activities as a neighbour who lives close by, you might drop both of them off at their activity and get the neighbour to return them. You can also engage the concept of double time (which I expand on in my chapter on valuing your time) so that you are achieving two goals at once; for example, connecting socially with friends while walking the dog. People who are good at leveraging their time often appear to others to be super organised or efficient. Of course, they have the same number of hours in the day as everyone else. They too are lazy, unfocussed and demotivated at times. But they have just learned to leverage their time well and take advantage of multiple opportunities to get things done within the limited time they have.

Leveraging time is a very important skill for entrepreneurs. Unlike employed "clock-watchers" who often engage in political tactics to make people think they are working harder than they are (for example, leaving their jackets on the back of the chair and their monitors on after they leave the office), leveraging your time will truly impact both your results and the quality of your life. So, get good at leverage and you will be repaid many times over through massively improved quality of your personal as well as business life.

Leverage is a popular concept in business that also allows you to multiply your time and accelerate your profits by using the money or resources of others. And what makes this possible is an exchange of value, or win-win, as it's often called. The famous American businessman and philanthropist John Rockefeller said, "I would rather earn 1% of 100 people's efforts than 100% of my own efforts." This summarises the leveraged approach to business.

Personally, I love leverage. I don't want to be someone who works twelve hours a day. And because I've got a family, I couldn't do that anyway because my life would become chaotic and I'd make everyone unhappy. So, I learned early in my entrepreneurial career to get good at leverage. If I hadn't, I probably would have given up trying to run a business years ago. Whether you have family commitments or not, I believe all entrepreneurs should use leverage to make their lives easier and more enjoyable. The all too common scenario of spinning plates and dropping balls when you're trying to do everything yourself is the reason leverage exists. If this resonates with you, it's probably time for you to step back from being overburdened and stressed out, and let leverage work for you, too.

The concept of entrepreneurial leverage can be a little theoretical and hard to understand if you haven't used it yet to grow and scale a business. So, rather than waffle on about theory, I'm going to give you four examples of real-life business leverage, involving the four main vehicles available to entrepreneurs: money, people, technology and systems.

The power of financial leverage

Here's an example of how financial leverage can work in business. A lot of property developers leverage both commercial bank finance and private equity finance to fund their projects. The private equity finance might come, for example, from professional investors who understand how to evaluate a property development deal, and who know and trust the developer. In return for providing the high-risk portion of the lending, developers are often prepared to give away up to half of the project profits, meaning gains for investors can be as high as 50% per annum (or even more) on their funds. Without equity investment, the developers will not be able to take on such projects, and without the projects, the investors would not be able to gain such great returns hands-free. This is something that I have considerable personal experience of, as investing in exactly this way was what kickstarted my own property business.

An example of using people leverage is affiliate or joint-venture marketing. Let's say you start a coaching business dedicated to improving profitability for underperforming small businesses. Rather than be the person who wades through endless lists, websites and financial information to find business owners who fit the profile of your target customer, and then writing to each of them individually, you could approach your accountants and tell them what you're doing. You persuade them, by way of a revenue split with you, to promote your services through email to any of their clients whose profits have declined in the past year, offering them a free consultation and action plan to address this issue. Again, note the win-win here. With very little effort or input, your accountants have gained a worthwhile share of your revenues and a way to differentiate themselves from their competition by providing a value-adding service to their clients. And you have gained access to exactly the type of pre-qualified clients you need to get your business off the ground.

The power of technology leverage

Let's now take the example of leveraging technology.

Technical disruption is without a doubt the fastest way for ordinary people, with limited resources at their disposal, to become rich and successful beyond their wildest dreams. For example, never before in history has there been the opportunity to cut out layers of wholesalers and middlemen and distribute a book like this easily, directly and affordably to thousands and even millions of customers. It is only made possible by leveraging channels such as Amazon, Kindle, Audible, or many of the other rapidly evolving content platforms on the web. Leveraging technology is a huge leveller. Regardless of age, looks, gender, sexual orientation, location or educational qualifications, wealth and success can be almost anyone's today, as long as they truly commit to the work it takes to generate it.

Technology today gives entrepreneurs like us access to markets that we could never have reached a decade ago. This creates unprecedented revenue opportunities. Whatever we want to achieve today, we can make it happen through the huge interconnectedness that is available to all of us who have a smartphone or computer. The opportunity is so huge that leveraging technology can feel scary to many. Because once we realise how easy it is, we'll have to adjust to the concept of massive growth leading to massive wealth, and this sets up a parallel challenge. Are you ready for this? Are you truly ready to leverage technology to distribute your product or service? Because if the answer is yes, you'll also have to ask yourself: am I/is it good enough? How will I/it stand out amongst my competition? What will (these millions of) others think or say about me, and how will I cope with the snipers, trolls and haters who want to tear me down? Then it becomes about the scariest concept of all for some, but also the sweetest thought: how will I deal with the wealth and success that will result as my "prize" for leveraging technology? My second book focusses on personal leadership and mindset, so if this is a route you are keen to investigate, I would recommend you read that one too.

The power of systems leverage

Finally, let's look at an example of leveraging systems. Franchises are excellent examples of leveraged systems. Think of Costa Coffee, for example, which provides complete consistency in products and customer experience across every one of its outlets. What no one realises is that some of the Costa outlets are owned by the company itself, but many are owned by independent franchisees. You can't tell the difference because they're all following the same system. Another favourite brand of mine is Premier Inn Hotels who guarantee a good night's sleep via their identical, bespoke beds that feature in exactly the same style of hotel room all across the UK. Leveraging systems that have already been developed and proven to work creates valuable shortcuts for businesses, and, in fact, this and a leveraged brand is how the franchise industry generates profits.

Whether you leverage money, people, systems or technology, you are establishing a win-win relationship that belongs to the mindset of success. So always look to leverage to help you get the most from your life and your business.

CHAPTER SIX:
Systemise for Success

Small business survival rates are as high as 90% after the first year of trading, but after five years, just four in ten will still exist. This is sometimes because the owners have been too busy to concentrate on the most important task of all—which is running their businesses profitably. They've spent too much time working IN their business rather than ON it. As Michael Gerber, author of the classic book on systems in business, The E-myth Revisited, said, "If your business depends on you, you don't own a business. You have a job, and it's the worst job in the world because you're working for a lunatic." You may think these words are harsh, but I think he said them because doing all the important work in a business, when you own it too, is enough to drive anyone insane! You need to spend time planning and executing its profitable growth instead so you can have a better business, and more importantly, a better life.

You're never irreplaceable

The worst belief that any business owner can have about themselves is that they're irreplaceable. This is a common but faulty notion that equates success with control. This mindset tends to happen when struggling entrepreneurs loosen the reins and find that disaster is the consequence. Whatever the problem—losing money or customers, a budget overrun, or sloppy work that's done by others—they arrive at the conclusion that this happened because they allowed someone else to do the work instead of them. So, in they go with gritted teeth, working eighteen-hour days and believing their active involvement in every aspect of the business is the only way to succeed. They become control freaks, driving everyone else as well as themselves crazy in the process.

Of course, what happens next is that instead of the business becoming more successful, it loses momentum and starts to unravel. The employees become disempowered. They feel that none of their ideas will be implemented, so they stop volunteering them. They start acting like children with an annoying parent, which in a way, they actually are! They disobey the rules when they think they can get away with it and pass the buck instead of being accountable for their actions. This also goes unnoticed and unchecked because there isn't a system in place for measuring and rewarding performance. Then the useful and valuable people leave and the coasters hang on, hiding behind their desks and doing their personal stuff on work time. The business owner becomes increasingly impatient, distressed and overwhelmed. The business isn't working, and he or she knows it. Why am I so sure of this? Because I've worked in these types of businesses and seen it myself many times over.

It's almost certain that if our struggling entrepreneur has a life partner or family, they too will be unhappy and resentful about the time their loved one is working IN their business. They didn't get into the relationship to be with an obsessional, underpaid and stressed-out workaholic, but that's what they've ended up with. Is it any wonder that, according to lawyers, entrepreneurs have one of the highest rates of divorce among all professions? It doesn't have to be this way, though, and systems are one of the most important solutions.

Small entrepreneurs usually start businesses because they have technical skills and expertise they want to profit from personally. If they're a chef, they open a restaurant. If they're a builder, they find a house to refurbish and sell. Perhaps they're a hairdresser who opens a salon or a designer that forms a small agency. Their solution to growth seems simple to begin with. It involves finding people to replicate their skills, so they get more hairdressers, designers, builders or chefs, and a handful of support staff to deal with admin and sales.

Put a plan in place

This is the myth that Michael Gerber refers to in his book. Business owners like these think their technical skills can also make them great at running a business, but they simply aren't. Once you open a business, you're not a freelancer or employee doing technical work any longer. Even if you're a solopreneur with a staff of one, you're now also heading up your own operations, finance, marketing, human resources, tech, and everything else involved in the running of a company. You need to put a plan in place for someone else to take care of these functions according to a high-level strategy you've evolved. That requires putting on a different hat—the hat of systematisation. You need to think of your business from day one as a franchise that has just established its first outlet. If you're a hairdresser or a chef, plan for a chain of twenty restaurants or salons. If you've formed a design agency, plan for twenty clients instead of one. If you're a builder, plan for the twenty-house site you're going to refurbish and sell. You don't have to execute this expansion from day one, but planning for it as if it were inevitable will get you in the mindset for growth. Since you can't be in twenty different places at once, you'll have to make decisions about the things you need to do for you to progressively remove yourself from the day-to-day running of your business so you can start to work ON this bigger entity rather than IN it.

If the thought of doing this makes you feel scared, remember that scaling successfully will always make your life easier and more enjoyable. You'll make more money too, which should be a big enough incentive in itself. The reason we all start businesses is because we want to do something meaningful that brings us material rewards. The more you leverage other people's expertise through having the right systems in place, the more satisfying both your life and your business will be. And the more choices you'll have about where to spend your time. When systems are working as they should, they can free you up to do the work you love and make your role feel effortless and joyful.

Look at Richard Branson, who I often like to reference. Through creating alliances with cash-rich partners, he's established multiple ventures in new sectors. He has more than 400 companies in music, entertainment, clothing, cosmetics, financial services, night clubs, train services, tour operations, health clubs, publishing, film industry, mobile phone services and even condoms. He prides himself on his ability to spot a gap in the market but admits that he's not a numbers or a details man, leaving the everyday running of his firms to a group of competent lieutenants. Through this, he finds the time to pursue multiple hobbies, be a loving father and family man, and has a huge amount of fun. He's a living testament to the power of systems.

Systems thinking creates a framework for seeing patterns of change in your business. When everybody is zoomed in on a single component, systems help you zoom out and look at the whole. When everybody is trying to analyse one component, systems help you analyse the relationships between them. Instead of relying on metrics, systems help you look at trends.

So have a plan, not just for your business, but for your life. This will make sure that your time is valued at a premium and that you don't waste it doing things that other people can do for you. Going back to the business owners who tried the hands-free approach and found it didn't work. Their businesses struggled for one reason only: themselves. Delegating responsibility to others before establishing systems that have been created to serve the needs and interests of the business leader, in other words, you, means that the personal agendas of others will prevail over yours. A leaderless business is doomed to fail because of clashing agendas creating chaos. So, whether you like it or not, you really only have one choice if you want your business to succeed: create systems to serve your goals every step of the way.

Systemise is not the same as delegate

Delegation is completely different to systemisation. Delegation is something everyone understands. If you don't like cleaning but you earn more than a cleaner, pay one to leverage your own time more usefully. You might tell them to hoover the stairs and clean the mirrors, but you probably wouldn't bother telling them exactly how you want them to do this or give them rewards and penalties for doing the job well or badly. Systemisation, in contrast, requires more detail. It's a high-level management function that requires clarity from you about both your personal goals and your vision for the business. It requires the ability to, step by step, create an implementable strategy that creates the same level of clarity for others. It's hard work and requires a lot of planning and thought in the beginning, but you need to see it as an investment that will earn you back valuable time and generate the results you want down the line.

As well as serving you, your systems need to motivate others. If they're done well, they will. We humans are hardwired to like certainty, which is what systems provide. They give people the freedom to operate within a box that balances freedom of choice with clearly defined goals, responsibilities and consequences for non-performance. If you're not sure where to start with systems, start with the most basic tasks in each individual department or function and create flow charts that show how things get done and by who. You can, of course, involve other people in this process, but it's important to remember that it all starts with you as the leader of your business and life. The more you put systems into practice, the more you'll be banking your future freedom and enjoyment. So, enjoy developing your systems and look forward to the time when you're enjoying the results, too.

CHAPTER SEVEN:
Be a Great Boss

In this chapter, I'm going to look at how you can be not just a better boss but a truly great boss. Being a great boss is one of the most important things you can do for your business and yourself as its leader. Bosses have the opportunity to create a culture that enriches the lives of others, which is immensely satisfying. Happy people are productive people, so it's also how to get the best results for your business.

Be tough but kind

To be a great boss, you have to be tough but kind. You have to protect the people who are creating ongoing value for you from the people whose vision for themselves no longer aligns with yours. So, a willingness to act quickly and decisively by shedding those who are not great for you or your business is also critical to your success. None of us like sacking people, but sometimes you'll be doing a truly wonderful thing for them. Think about Huda Kattan, a make-up artist, beauty blogger, entrepreneur and founder of the very successful business Huda Beauty. Huda ranks ahead of Beyonc and Kim Kardashian on the list of America's richest self-made women. She says, "When I lost my job, I was like, 'F*** all of this.' It changed my life. It was the catalyst to becoming who I am." If you have to sack someone, who are you to say you are not helping another budding entrepreneur find their true mission in life?

Managing people isn't always easy, although the reason for this is often the issues managers are having with themselves. If you have personal problems that you've not dealt with, or if you're simply unfulfilled in your life and work, dealing with others can create uncomfortable and even unbearable feelings for you. This can spill over into behaviour that upsets others and makes you one of those bosses that employees dread facing.

When feeling the pressure, many bosses overreact and become volatile with others, thinking they can get away with it because they wield power over them. This is the fastest way to create distrust, resentment and disengagement. So, a key goal for every boss should be to achieve emotional self-mastery. This doesn't mean acting like an unemotional robot, which makes it hard for others to see you for the real and lovely human being you are. It means being able to own and express your feelings calmly and with confidence, which inspires others to be open and courageous around you, too.

Know yourself

So, the first rule of managing people well is to know and understand yourself. This concept has been around as long as people were thinking about life. "Knowing yourself is the beginning of all wisdom," said the ancient Greek philosopher and scientist Aristotle. "To find yourself, think for yourself," said Socrates, who was born in 470 BC and is considered to have been the founder of Western philosophy. "To thine own self be true," said the most famous playwright ever, William Shakespeare.

Knowing yourself is not about the list of things you like to do in life. It's also not about your accomplishments or success. That's pandering to the ego, the part of us that only has two needs: to acquire praise and to deflect fear. When you think of yourself as a list of interests and accomplishments, and when your identity is tied up with your financial status or position in life, you're in the world of average people. "Averages", as you might call them, are where the bad bosses are found. "Averages" don't practise habits of self-awareness, so if they're employing people, they're more likely to behave badly or appear emotionally closed to others.

How can you achieve emotional self-mastery? It's simple, but it's not easy. It requires building habits of self-reflection and awareness into your life on a daily basis, which gives you the space to identify your feelings and ask where they're coming from. There are many ways to do this. Some do it through prayer or meditation, some do it by going for long walks alone, and others write in diaries. Some reach out to trusted friends, mentors or their home team, who make a habit of listening rather than advising.

The purpose of reflection is to throw the spotlight back on yourself, because when you have a difficult or complicated feeling, it's always more about you than the other person. Someone else's behaviour may have triggered the reaction or feeling, but you're looking in the wrong place if you're attributing either judgment or blame to them. You need to instead ask yourself what's going on within you to make you overreact or get upset. Moments of peace, like walks and meditation, can be good for this, but they're what I call "level-one check-ins". They're most suitable for people with lives that already have space and comfort in them.

If you're managing people through change or growth, your space and comfort levels will be massively squeezed. That's when you need to progress to level two, which is your check-in with insightful others. Your check-ins during times of challenge need to be with those who can understand, listen patiently and relate precisely to what you're saying. If you're managing a team of people, and you're expressing your fears and challenges to someone who's never been in that position, you'll struggle to get quality feedback and you'll feel frustrated and disconnected as a consequence.

Don't rely on your friends or life partner to give you the support you need at times like this, as this can drain the positive energy from your relationship with them. It's not their place to support you with your business challenges. Far better to get the help elsewhere and come back to them refreshed and as the best possible version of yourself. This is why mentors, as opposed to therapists or coaches, are so valuable. Find someone who's been in your shoes, who understands the challenges of managing businesses and people, and who's done it successfully themselves. This also meets your need to grow and develop, which is just as important for you as for your employees. So, don't go it alone; you'll always be stronger with the right person by your side.

The other aspect of being a great boss is to really care about other people. Take an interest in your employees' lives. Give them your time and attention, even if it's only a few minutes every other day. Ask them how they're doing and how their families are. And when they answer, react to what they say rather than changing the subject back to you or what you want them to do for you. Catch them doing something right and compliment them on it instead of watching out for what they're doing wrong. You'll find it easier, of course, to give them this positive attention when you're not overwhelmed yourself. And this is where your mentor comes in. The support you receive will help you give your employees the consistent care they need through the good as well as the tough times.

The four principles of managing others

Here are my top four principles for managing others. **Step One** is to establish an empowered culture, putting care and connection first. Lead by example, showing that your business is a place where courage, emotional openness and independent thinking are rewarded. Where mistakes are celebrated as a sign of trying, and blame, judgement and power plays are discouraged.

If someone's struggling, invite them to come to you and help them resolve the issue. If they could have tackled it by themselves, tell them so they will feel empowered to deal with similar challenges in future. Help them share and implement their ideas. Give them goals and standards of behaviour that can be taught, measured and evaluated. Demonstrate, through your own conduct, that the best route to success is helping others succeed.

Step Two is to have tough conversations. Take a deep breath and prepare to go outside your comfort zone, because you will. But it's worth it. These conversations are the ones that will lead to lasting, positive change in your business. Discourage the cultural norm of "nice and polite", which causes a lack of clarity, poor trust and engagement and increases problematic behaviour. If someone isn't taking responsibility for their performance or is trying to shift blame or accountability onto someone else, give it to them straight.

I've been in business environments for as long as I can remember. I've seen all the best leaders and managers do this. You don't need to be unkind, harsh or angry. Be firm, no matter how uncomfortable it feels, and make it a rule not to say things behind a person's back that you wouldn't say to their face. Watch for others doing this, too. Discourage gossip, side meetings and the bitchy discussions that marginalise some and let others have power that is disproportionate to their role. It's also really important to quickly tackle bad apples or those who are a destabilising influence. Make it clear that this type of behaviour is unacceptable in your business and give them appropriate consequences for violating the standards you have worked so hard to set.

Step Three is to learn about and work with other peoples' values. In small companies, opportunities for career progression can be limited, but this may not be what matters to your employees. Perhaps they care more about flexible working hours, acquiring new skills, or the opportunity to earn high commissions. You won't know until you ask each of them individually. So, make it a habit to check-in personally with others, as well as yourself, and ask them how you can serve them better. If it becomes all about the money, recognise that your leadership is the issue. Sometimes, on the other hand, people are just not a good fit for you and your business anymore, so don't automatically pander to their demands. Instead, ask them what else matters and you'll often get to the truth.

Step Four is to bring your emotions to discussions, which encourages others to bring theirs in turn. Rather than addressing the fears and concerns that people have in times of change, many bosses spend their time managing the problematic behaviour that results. Learn to speak from the heart. This doesn't mean indiscriminately sharing everything or seeking reassurance and comfort from your employees. That's being needy, and it is inappropriate behaviour from a boss. Understand what's disturbing you, as well as others, at any given time. Share your feelings about this and tell others what you think both you and they can do to improve emotional and practical outcomes. Here's the type of thing you could say: "I feel sad, both for myself and for you, that your hard work and efforts weren't appreciated by our client. But disappointments and setbacks are a valuable part of running any business. The lessons we've learned will make us more successful in future, so let's look at how we could get it right next time."

If the issue is something that's out of your control or can't be resolved—for example, a declining economy—be real about the truth of this and remain a positive, loving and encouraging presence for your employees. Remember that courage, like every emotion, is contagious. You can't be courageous without also being vulnerable. They go together like sausage and mash, strawberries and cream, and all the other things in life that exist in perfect pairs. So, get strength from mentors, which will help you let others in. Show your employees you have feelings too and you'll get the respect and loyalty you deserve.

CHAPTER EIGHT:
How to Discipline and Fire

Although we'd all love a perfect world and a perfect business, real life isn't set up for perfection, and this is certainly true when it comes to hiring employees. You can be the most diligent employer in the world and do everything to the best of your ability. Prepare a well-thought-out strategy and role, ask someone all the right interview questions, obtain references, check out experience and qualifications, perform psychometric and skills tests, and introduce them to your team for a second opinion and interviews, all before you commit. You can offer them flexible benefits, bonus schemes and career paths. A great culture and a thriving business. None of this insures against bad employees.

Bad is, of course, a judgmental word, and it should be said that people themselves are rarely bad. However, they can become bad for you and your business. In other words, harm rather than help it, and you need to act quickly if this is the case. Even great bosses recruit people who are either a poor fit or not up to the task. So as long as you're in business, dealing with them is always going to be part of your job.

Employees can look like a great fit to begin with. They can make a good start and then something starts to slide. They become disruptive, difficult with colleagues, lazy, unwilling to learn or adapt to your organisational culture and rules. Sadly, sometimes they simply struggle with the demands of the work or have personal or psychological difficulties that are impacting their ability to do it.

Don't bury your head in the sand

If you have a difficult employee, the worst thing you can do is bury your head in the sand and hope the problem will go away by itself, because it won't. And the longer it's left, the worse it will affect your other employees—the ones who are creating genuine value for you.

Before you fire someone, you have to make sure it's not because of your weak leadership. Aim to make your business not just a good place to work, but a great place to work. A place where you always prioritise the wellbeing of your employees. Produce a handbook stating your commitment to this, as well as the rules and standards you expect employees to abide by. If you have a small business, this doesn't have to be complicated. It can be fun and light-hearted, defining the mission, culture and character of your company. But it should also clarify acceptable and unacceptable behaviour, the action that's taken if your rules are broken, and the procedures you have in place to deal with poor performance and conduct. There are many free resources on the internet that can help you with this.

Make sure you or your managers have identified KRAs (key results areas) and KPIs (key performance indicators) for each employee so they have benchmarks against which their performance can be measured. Have proper reviews rather than informal chats and make a note of what was discussed and any actions that were agreed. Ask them about their goals and aspirations and put a plan in place to address them. Be the best boss you can by catching people doing things right. Give them your time, attention and interest, even if they are very junior in your business. Establish a culture where blame and lack of accountability are discouraged and courage and risk-taking are rewarded. Operate an open-door policy around problems as well as opportunities, and show people you care by fully addressing the issues they bring to you.

Employee engagement is so critical to your company's success. When you invest in your employees, they'll become invested in your business success, and that's a great way to boost your profits.

Employees who feel valued tend to communicate and collaborate more. They report a high level of satisfaction, have higher levels of productivity and generate a happier atmosphere. This means that when you're not around, rather than whinging or slacking off, they'll be getting on with the work and having fun with each other.

Emotional mastery

It's easy in the good times for bosses to feel relaxed and act graciously, but too many either hide away or start throwing their weight around when times get tough. Emotional mastery is a key feature of strong leadership. This doesn't mean being stoical during the difficult times, pretending feelings don't count or dismissing problems as if they're irrelevant to the bigger picture. Rather, it's engaging your heart and soul with the challenges both you and your employees are facing. Showing them you understand and care about their experience and leading by being a positive and encouraging presence for them.

Assuming you've done all of this and you still have problems with someone, you first need to be clear about your legal responsibilities and adopt the procedures that protect you from claims of unfair dismissal. Lawyers and human resource specialists can advise you of this if you have the budget for it, but if you don't, there's a lot of information freely available to support small businesses such as yours.

There needs to be a sequential series of meetings over a period of time starting with a performance improvement plan to set some clear targets. If the employee doesn't meet these, a review needs to happen. After that, it may be necessary to issue a verbal or written warning. This process can be repeated, which might result in a final warning and a last chance to turn things around. If there's no improvement after the final written warning and you have to fire someone, you should call a meeting with the employee and somebody representing them. Remind them of what's led up to this point, their failure to improve performance, and inform them of their dismissal in accordance with your disciplinary procedure. Your employee should be given the opportunity to appeal within 14 days. They should also be given a letter confirming the dismissal and the right to appeal, the time period for appeal and who to appeal to. The reason why poor performance must be addressed systematically is because you as an employer have an obligation to behave ethically. Before employment law insisted on fair practice, employees would be horribly exploited and discarded without any consideration for the impact on their lives.

The consequences of firing

Sacking an employee is a serious matter. Apart from the loss of income, there can be a stigma attached, which can affect their personal life and future job prospects. So, try in all instances to be objective and kind. You owe it to yourself as well as others to behave with high integrity and consideration for another human being, however angry or disappointed you may be feeling with them. Even if you feel your employee hates you and wants to harm your efforts to build a great business, you shouldn't take it personally. Some people just have an issue with men, women, tall people, slim people, popular or successful people, or authority figures, and work is a convenient place to act out their dysfunction. It's never about you unless you let it be.

Rather than go through sequential performance plans and warnings, you can sometimes have an off-the-record conversation with senior employees and strike a deal. For example, you can allow them the dignity of resigning as long as they don't do anything to damage your reputation or business afterwards. It's a good idea to speak to your lawyer or HR specialist before this type of conversation, as if someone's pregnant, for example, this would still be perceived as discrimination. When a deal of this type is struck, both parties will normally enter into a settlement agreement with the employee being obliged to obtain independent legal advice.

Sacking someone is never a happy task. It will also impact you emotionally, even if the employee has been warned repeatedly and has had every chance to improve. It is someone's livelihood after all, and it's tough to take paying work away from another human being. Remembering the times that I had to sack someone, I vividly recall the sadness, fear and sometimes hostility in their eyes. It's tough, so if you have to do it, make sure you get powerful help and support for you, too.

As hard as firing someone is, having the right people in your business is absolutely critical to your entrepreneurial success. Holding high standards and expecting people to meet them should be one of your most important goals. You don't fire people on a whim or without warning. You tell them what they need to do to keep their job, and if they can't or choose not to make those changes, that's not your responsibility. Remember that being fired can sometimes have an incredibly positive impact on people, too. It can be the wake-up call that changes their direction in life or helps them do better in the future. Not being the right match for you is ok. Your life, as well as theirs, goes on.

CHAPTER NINE:
Be a Producer Not a Consumer

I've recently been listening on Audible to two books on the subject of entrepreneurship by a US entrepreneur and author called MJ DeMarco. The first is called Millionaire Fast Lane, and the second is called Unscripted. If you're serious about growing and scaling a fabulously profitable business fast, you should definitely read or listen to them. I loved these books so much that I decided to dedicate this whole chapter to one of DeMarco's concepts.

The concept I'm referring to is how the route to rapid wealth requires a shift in focus from being a consumer to a producer. A producer is an inventor of original products or experiences that are capable of delivering value to the customers they serve. Many of the wealthiest and most successful entrepreneurs in the world have done just this. By creating value for millions, or sometimes billions, they have created millions or billions for themselves. Of course, this isn't the only way to get rich, but this is the fast-lane entrepreneurial method. In contrast, systemised businesses developed by others, like franchises, multilevel marketing systems and financial products associated with the stock market, only create wealth at the source for most people.

Some entrepreneurs do well from investing time or money with franchises and network marketing companies. But this is a slower and less profitable route to success. To put it in specific terms, if you're the creator and owner of Baskin Robbins, Europcar, Intercontinental Hotels or Utility Warehouse, which are successful franchises, or Herbalife, Amway or Mannatech, which are successful network marketing companies, you're going to be massively wealthier than others who are simply delivering on your brand, products and systems.

What is a producer?

A producer is someone with a vision and original idea. Someone who has the stamina and self-belief to translate this into a brand, process and system that pushes it out to the consumer. If you want to create millions fast, this is a great way to do it.

Of course, there's nothing wrong with a mix-and-match approach to life. We all need to pay our bills, and a lot of us have families to support too. So, plenty of entrepreneurs have a second or even third string to their bow. You may be working in a job and starting a business as a "side hustle". Perhaps you've got a systemised business going in another sector and want to get started with something new. Perhaps you're a student who's devoting some of your time to study. Or a consultant with ideas you want to bring to a wider audience. The reality is that the world we inhabit has changed dramatically, and with powerful internet marketing tools at our disposal, fast-lane entrepreneurship is genuinely an option for all of us—even those with minimal resources to spare. All you have to do is develop something people will want to buy and be willing to put in the work to deliver it to them. Oh, and if you don't think fast-lane entrepreneurship involves work, be prepared for twelve-hour days, seven days a week, with an intense focus on your ONE goal, because that's what it takes to get a fast-lane business off the ground. In the beginning, this may involve working at a day job or the equivalent while working all hours through the evening, night and weekend. The four-hour working week and millionaire lifestyle is the by-product of a mature business that started with massive effort and sacrifice.

It's not easy to make the shift from being a consumer to a producer, but it's certainly possible for most of us. You'll need to start by coming up with an idea you feel really excited about. Then, evaluate and test your market until you can shape an offer that genuinely meets its needs. You'll need to dedicate yourself to the process and develop a mindset of success, the power of which is something that many entrepreneurs struggle with. Think about the words of Winston Churchill who said, "Success is not final, failure is not fatal. It's the courage to continue that counts." Failure is the only route to success. Failure always needs to be seen as feedback—a critical part of getting things right. We can't be crushed if we put effort into something that doesn't work because each failure takes us closer to what is going to work, even when it doesn't seem like it.

What is a consumer?

Which brings me back to the title of this chapter: "Be a producer, not a consumer". Let's now look at the role of the consumer. A consumer lives by the law of averages and social norms. He or she is a person who, at the end of a short-ish working day, settles down to watch TV or consume media, participates in hobbies such as video games or pool shooting, engages with social media for purely personal reasons, or visits a bar or pub to drink with his or her mates. Note these are activities that will not make our consumer mentally or physically healthier, improve their knowledge of the world, or create value for others who matter to them like their spouse or children. In other words, they're people who help themselves to many hours of doing nothing much.

Consumers often work hard at their jobs, so I'm not suggesting they don't deserve downtime. But they're choosing an average life of average values that average people understand. I'm not criticising them for doing this; plenty of people don't care about fast-track entrepreneurship, which is, of course, completely fine. This book isn't for them. In fact, it's also not for you if you're one of these people and, for some curious reason, still reading. People who want to make the shift from consumer to producer, however, need to find a tolerable but acceptable balance between pleasure in the now and the deferred gratification that comes from the right effort, at the right time, and in the right place to create exponential success down the line.

Whenever the effort required to build a successful business feels like hard going, think of this quote: "Six months of hardcore focus and alignment can put you five years ahead in life. Never underestimate the power of consistency and desire."

Your difference is your value

What's this got to do with people? The very act of being—or trying to be—a successful entrepreneur sets you apart from the majority of the people you will encounter in life. And I just want to encourage you in this respect. It really is okay to be different, to want more, and to strive for more than the average people you know. But there will be times when you become aware of your difference. People will think you're strange and behave in ways that make you realise it. Because "averages" don't understand entrepreneurship, they will compare you to people who have a mature business that they've been monetising for years and secretly label you a loser. It can be hard to maintain relationships in the face of this, and this is where you need a home team consisting of entrepreneurial peers or mentors who will encourage and support you as you move steadily towards your vision and goals.

Producers are the innovators of our world. They're stubbornly searching for ways to translate their original business ideas into what MJ calls "value vouchers" for the people they serve. In reality, that means you must never give up on your dreams until you've reached the level of success that you truly want. Every day, no matter what's going on, producers make sacrifices and dedicate time to moving forward with their entrepreneurial goals and ideas. Patiently, and with the knowledge that while others are consuming the first-world lifestyle benefits their income affords them, they are experiencing the setbacks, deprivation and false starts that are crafting their amazing future.

CHAPTER TEN:
Affiliate and Joint Venture Success

Affiliates and joint ventures are popular forms of leverage. Leverage is one of my favourite business concepts because it helps you achieve otherwise unachievable growth through the money, time, skills, contacts or resources of others. The reason leverage is such a powerful strategy is because it creates benefit for both parties and its success depends on maintaining a two-way exchange of value.

Why entrepreneurs joint venture

Let's start by looking at joint ventures. Joint ventures are people or businesses who come together for the purpose of reaching a common goal. This can be to accelerate growth, increase productivity, or generate new profit. Sometimes, it's for all of these reasons. Successful joint ventures have a lot to do with emotional intelligence as well as business strategy. This is because joint ventures are made by people, between people, and the quality of that relationship is a key factor influencing its success. I love this strategy because it's low risk and reversible. It can be a stepping stone to a full business partnership or a short-term "suck it and see". Let's look at this further.

Take the example of a property investor or developer. They have the skills and expertise to run multiple projects, but their growth is held back by a lack of capital. Therefore, they will look for a cash-rich investor to joint venture with. The investor has no desire to tie up his or her time managing and exiting property deals but is motivated by the opportunity to achieve financial growth hands-free. Both partners have a common goal, which is to make money from property. If one deal goes well, they'll proceed to the next. If it doesn't, they'll part ways and the investor will simply get his or her capital returned (at least, they should do. As for the how, just get in touch as this is something I specialise in). It's simple and easy for everyone to understand.

Another example of a joint venture is a business that lacks expertise in something that their clients are asking for. Buying in knowledge in a non-core area can be risky because we "don't know what we don't know". Making the wrong choice because you're out of your own skillset can lead to increased overhead without the desired returns. So instead, the business can choose the lower risk route of joint venturing with another company that already has a successful product or service they need. This is how joint ventures can deepen and extend your offer to clients and prevent them from going elsewhere. And it's so powerful because it fulfils the first rule of a successful business: satisfying the customer profitably.

The law of win-win has to be observed for joint ventures to work, so there should be clear agreements from the start that address any existing or future competitive areas, as well as defining financial incentives such as commissions or bonuses. This helps build trust and increases the likelihood that the joint venture will be successful.

The same type of value doesn't have to be created for both partners in a joint venture. In our previous example, one company might want to keep their employees busy and well paid, whereas the other might look to achieve fee revenues for managing the new service. Joint ventures are infinitely flexible, but they have to be properly thought through to work. And I've seen some massive mistakes in this respect.

When my design business was bought by a US communications group, we were told we had to build client referrals and joint-venture arrangements between us and the other European design companies they also had bought. So, involving a lot of effort and expense, we were made to attend the HQ of one of these companies every month in Rome, Stockholm, Paris, Madrid, Amsterdam, Berlin; all the major

European cities. I did manage to have some fun (Of course! Who wouldn't when staying in top design hotels in great cities with a bunch of fun-seeking European business owners), but we all would have had a lot more had this not been such a badly thought through exercise.

We were all graphic design companies. Some of us specialised in packaging, some in TV, digital or corporate identity, but since we were all on earn-outs (meaning we had to generate the high profits that justified us being bought in the first place), we had huge price tags and targets on our heads. We would grab any design work we were offered, in or outside our niche, as long as there was profit in it. Not a single referral happened. After a while, predictably, the whole thing fell apart, which is a familiar story for hastily put together M&A (mergers and acquisition) deals.

Why entrepreneurs create affiliates

The difference between an affiliate and a joint venture is that affiliates are sales and marketing arrangements between two companies rather than any other exchange of value. They're particularly popular in the digital space. An example of this is when an online retailer—for example, a seller of vitamins and supplements—pays a commission to an external website, a healthcare site, or Amazon for traffic or sales generated from its referrals.

The advantages of the affiliate marketing business model are clear. It creates the opportunity to sell stock without having the costs or responsibilities of manufacturing, buying or storing it. Affiliates with a strong social following, also known as influencers, can even receive freebies from advertisers looking to boost their brand awareness.

Online groups and platforms such as Facebook and LinkedIn are good examples of affiliate marketing. By posting valuable content, you help the platform or groups to promote their own brand. In turn, they help you establish credibility in your particular area of expertise. There are also many real-world or non-digital affiliate opportunities that are especially suitable for locally based businesses. There are several different forms of shop window available to you. If you pay a small fee or referral commission, you can advertise in many places from the notice board in the church hall to the leaflets you place in the doctor's waiting area, to advertising signage on a car or van. Even a small sticker placed in a prominent position in the rear window of your car with a few words and your URL can help attract potential customers. Networking events are also a form of affiliate opportunity. You pay an entry fee to wander around and chat to likely customers, hand them your business card, and establish some face-to-face rapport, which all increase the chance that they'll buy from you.

Whether your affiliate marketing is online or offline, the key to success is finding the right prospects in the right place and at the right time to build your business. Then, you can pay either an upfront or referral fee or commission to the people or businesses that are providing them. It's a good idea to track the results of each affiliate marketing method you use, which will help you see which methods give you the best return on your investment.

Since I want to support you becoming the very best versions of yourselves, as well as enjoy the best relationships along the way, I'd like to share my people-centric insight on joint ventures and affiliate marketing.

These arrangements, as stated already, only work because there's a mutual exchange of value. In the digital space, this can be seen as a set-and-forget automated and systemised strategy where you're not required to have high levels of one-to-one communication with the people behind the product. This means you can make a decision pretty easily with the right research. The main effort needs to go into communicating with your employees, customers and wider audience, as well as evolving your personal brand and offer.

Choosing the right partnerships, avoiding the wrong ones

In the non-digital world of joint ventures, this is different. Often, some fairly intense personal engagement is required. And when this is the case, it's a good idea to get to know a prospective joint-venture partner over a period of time. For example, for several months, involving multiple forms of communication and at least eight meetings of different types (e.g. coffee/dinner) in different places to monitor and assess their experience, ethics and behaviour. Remember, they'll be assessing you at the same time, so bring awareness to your own conduct during this period and ask yourself how you'd feel to be on the receiving end of it!

The reason for meeting in different places is that being on familiar territory is more comfortable for people, so this can help them hide their less desirable traits. It also gives you a chance to check out any power plays by noting whether they're prepared to come to you or they want you to do the running. Always do your due diligence, but don't rely on it. I've personally seen so many nightmares that result from people jumping in feet first after a clean bill of due diligence. Remember the old saying: "Marry in haste, repent in leisure." And know that this rule applies to business too.

Joint ventures are a form of business partnership, and I want you to avoid wasting time on the wrong ones. The best way to do this is to hold back on commitment until you know what you're letting yourself in for. If someone's forcing the pace, either personally or professionally, step back to the same degree. Regardless of the opportunity that seems to jump out at you, you must be allowed the time to work out whether they're genuinely capable of creating the type of partnership you're looking for. Everyone possesses every character trait, be it positive or negative, and you're no exception. So don't expect perfection from yourself or others, but aim instead to understand where their weaknesses are—and yours too—and ask yourself whether the interface is comfortable enough for you to proceed.

Get to know the people who gather around your prospective joint-venture partner, because you'll be taking them on too. Who are their partners in business as well as life, and how will those relationships impact on the one you have with them? If you've always been a good judge of character, and if all your relationships have worked out well and brought you happiness, you'll have confidence in your choices around people. But we can all make mistakes, so don't be too trusting. For most of us, the opposite is true. People can cause havoc and great pain in your life if you make the wrong choices. So go slow, be generous and open, and watch how your prospective partner reacts.

If their response is to take from you without investing in return, you'll know that that's how they'll be in your partnership. If you're diligent and attentive in your communications, and they are lazy and uncommunicative, ditto. People leave clues early in any relationship; it's your job is to pick up on them. This is the thing that will bring you happiness and real-world joint venture success.

CHAPTER ELEVEN:
Why You Must Master Your Time

"Either you run the day, or the day runs you." Jim Rohn

"Time isn't a commodity, something you pass around like a cake. Time is the substance of life. When anyone asks you to give your time, they're really asking for a chunk of your life." Antoinette Bosco, journalist and author.

In this chapter, I'm going to explain why the way you treat your time is one of the most important considerations for everyone. And I'm going to give you five ways to use your time more efficiently.

Unlike money, which, if you're an entrepreneur, you'll naturally be setting out to create, time is a finite resource and the most precious one of all. We all have relatively short lives in which to fulfil our purpose and create a legacy for ourselves and others. So, we must prioritise time. Time gives us the freedom to dedicate ourselves to what really matters to us. It's the ultimate form of wealth, a luxury which material possessions can never replace. This is why slavery is such cruelty; it denies its victims both the time and the money to enjoy life in a way that is meaningful to them.

I was introduced to the idea of double time by one of my business and property mentors, Rob Moore. I love this concept. It involves merging everyday chores with business, and through this making every moment you have count. Rob takes it to the limits, legendarily having his hair cut by a mobile hairdresser when he's in board meetings. He taught me to use my train and car journeys, dog walks, waits at the doctor and in the hospital, queues in the supermarket and other "empty" time, to either enrich my mind or work on my business. For example, I rarely take a car journey alone without listening to books on Audible. I make phone calls when I'm walking the dog, and I take my smartphone everywhere so I can work whenever I'm waiting. This also stops me from filling my head with irrelevant (to my life) yet addictive media like Hello Magazine, upsetting news events, which can throw me off balance and get me worried about the world, or other mind-numbing trivia like radio chat. Rob is also a great advocate of time tracking to see where your invested time versus spent time goes. To obtain results in business, you need to make sure you are investing the maximum time into your IGTs (income generating tasks) and leveraged property and business systems. But you also need to invest time into your health, family and personal connections and priorities. We all need downtime, fun and relaxation, and having this discipline is great because it frees you up more for these.

How entrepreneurs waste time

So let's move on to looking at the mistakes many entrepreneurs make when it comes to their use of time, and how better habits and systems can make your finite time work better for you. A common way that entrepreneurs drain their time is through lack of clarity. One of my favourite sayings is, "Always be clear about your purpose or others will use you for theirs." What are your goals in life and business? And what are you going to do every day to move them forward? The reason it's important to ask yourself this is because it puts you in the driving seat of your time. Once you've decided what you're going to do every day and completed it, your work is done. And everything else, including the demands others place upon you, is an optional extra.

Some think it helps to put a real or theoretical hourly price on your head. If you're mathematically orientated and into business KPIs, you can use a system called ROTI (return on time invested) to work this out. Otherwise, if you don't want to do this, just tell yourself you're worth £100 or £200hr, or whatever price you decide to value your time at. Then carefully monitor your efforts to see how much others are costing you. It's human nature for people to try to use others to do tasks they can't be bothered to do themselves. And if you're not watching out for this natural but entirely selfish streak in people, you'll find yourself doing them. Develop a healthy self-interest, and make sure your time invested is a win-win for you as well as others. If they expect you to go on making sacrifices for their benefit, without either paying you what you're worth or investing time in what matters to you in return, recognise they're using you and move on.

Many think lazy people make poor entrepreneurs, but they're wrong. Lazy people can be very creative when it comes to organising their time. They tend not to waste it on unnecessary activities and get straight to the point. A lazy entrepreneur will always look for ways to automate and optimise all the repetitive processes in their businesses, as there is nothing more annoying for them than their time being wasted on low-level work that others could do. It's easier for lazy people than their hard-working and conscientious peers to prioritise their own goals instead of focussing on those imposed by other people. Because their heads aren't filled with to-do lists or the agendas of others, they tend to be more creative and enterprising. A lazy person with a burning purpose can be a fantastic time warrior. Let's hear it for lazy people, yeahhhh!!

Some people, as well as businesses, find it helpful to use a time-tracking app such as Toggl to plan their time and see where it goes. It helps them stay on track and see very clearly when they've been pulled away from their planned tasks. I allocate half of my working day (roughly) to my property interests and half to my content creation and training business. I don't track my personal time as I don't feel the need to right now, but if you're quite geeky, you may find it fun to do this and see where those valuable hours go.

Step into your zone of genius

It's always better to spend as much time as possible in your zone of brilliance or genius rather than in your zone of incompetence, which as well as wasting your time will make you feel worse about yourself. Your time is too precious to spend it feeling bad unnecessarily. Don't spend hours trying to fix the printer if you're capable of earning three times as much per hour doing what you do best. Get a printer engineer in to fix it, reserving your precious time for the high-value tasks you do so well.

If you're a parent, watch out. Your children can be massive time stealers if you let them. Being a doormat is neither dignified nor noble. You owe it to them as well as yourself to show them that you have time and attention for them, but that they must respect your time, too. And what you use this for—fulfilling your life's purpose and delivering on your goals—is not up for debate, guilt-tripping or negotiation. If you're a wife or girlfriend, watch out. Men will often steal your time if you let them. Leaving you to work AND do all the domestic and childcare chores while they enjoy non-negotiable hobbies, social lives and interests while building exciting and rewarding careers or businesses of their own. This is an absolute fact for many women; it has been tracked and measured all over the world. It sometimes works the other way around too. I know one guy who worked long hours as an accountant all week. He looked after his young children all weekend while his wife went clubbing on both Friday and Saturday night. She spent the rest of the weekend either sleeping off hangovers, or spending the money he earned shopping for clothes with her friends. Unsurprisingly, they're now divorced.

Another way in which entrepreneurs drain their time is through going it alone. If you try to do everything yourself, even the tasks you hate and are bad at, you will not only give yourself a bad life, but you will also find yourself falling into bed each night exhausted and drained. Get good at leverage. Decide what you're going to do and get rid of the rest. Even as a solopreneur, you need to embrace a CEO attitude. Find a way to outsource those unwanted tasks, whether it's through employing teenagers at school, virtual or local assistants, joint-venture or affiliate partners or paid professionals. Just don't do it all yourself.

The third way entrepreneurs drain their time is through travel. The concept of meeting for coffee is very popular in property circles, but coffee often entails a car journey in traffic or going on public transport. Only agree to a meeting if a Skype call won't do. If you have several meetings, try to group them together, getting others to come to you if possible. Of course, there are times when face to face is really important, especially if you're trying to close a deal, develop a partnership, or service a client with attention and focus, but for everything else, just be ruthless and say no. When the famous media executive Greg Dyke ran ITV, he was famous for only having stand-up meetings that were scheduled to last for no longer than fifteen minutes. That's an example of someone who values his time.

The fourth way entrepreneurs drain their times is through distractions like social media, gaming, unscheduled phone calls and so on. If you're prone to distractions like this, it's probably because you're not giving yourself enough breaks. You need to intersperse periods of intense focus and activity with scheduled breaks to do whatever makes you feel good. For me, social media mostly represents work, so I like to go for a walk out in nature, have scheduled calls with friends, go to the gym, find a new song on Spotify to add to my playlists or browse the internet for random stuff such as cute raccoon videos. But I try to make this time-limited and conscious (most of the time, as I'm only human too, ha-ha!) and then I go back to work.

The fifth way entrepreneurs drain their time is through not prioritising properly. I used to dive into the day by answering emails and then realised that by doing this, I was putting other people's agendas before my own. So, think about the order of your day and put your own agenda first, after any practical commitments such as taking kids to school. Also recognise that it's ok to ignore people sometimes—just make sure you notify them that you're only available at certain times or through certain channels. You don't have to be always on tap, 24/7.

Prioritise and have a system

If you're interested in studying this subject further, author and entrepreneur Brian Tracy wrote a great book about time management called Eat That Frog!: Get More Of The Important Things Done Today. If you're launching into the day answering emails and taking calls, you are dancing to someone else's tune. You have to make time for emails and calls, of course, but place them lower on your list of priorities than "eating your frog", which is a metaphor for tackling the biggest and most important task for you to accomplish in that day. The one you are most likely to procrastinate on, but which will also have the greatest positive impact on your life. As Mark Twain once said, "If it's your job to eat a frog, it's best to do it first thing in the morning. And if it's your job to eat two frogs, it's best to eat the biggest one first." Eating the frog means to get on and do it; otherwise, the frog will eat you, meaning that you'll end up procrastinating and feeling bad for the whole day.

The best way to set up a system for this is to decide the night before what your "frog" is for the next day. You may have some lesser frogs, but just decide on your main one. Then treat yourself after you've "eaten" it with something that nurtures your soul and spirit, whatever that may be. It could be a jog, yoga or meditation, a walk with the dog in nature, a blast of AC/DC, a spot of online shopping, watching a motivational video or doing something else that makes you happy. The important thing is that it sends you into the rest of the day in the best frame of mind and ready to take on other your priorities. I try to begin my day with the "frog" that needs to be eaten. Then I go to my most inspiring and rewarding activity, my writing, which I try to do for at least an hour. After this, I can address the other tasks, or lesser frogs, as I think of them. It's easy to do this once you have a clear vision for your life. So, as I often say, start with the end in mind. People will use up your time to help themselves if they can, sometimes without even realising. Always be respectful and considerate of others but remain firm. Take all these principles on board and you'll be well on your way to achieving mastery of your time.

CHAPTER TWELVE:
Create Value and Wealth Will Follow

In this chapter, I'm going to look at how success in business is achieved through the creation of value. And I'm going to give you a five-step system to generate value that takes you from the creation of a business idea through feedback loops that improve your product or service and deliver the ultimate in customer satisfaction.

The 20th-century value model

Traditionally, value creation in business has been associated with industrial scale, revolving around mass production and systemised, repeatable tasks. This is a 20th-century, manufacturing-based business model. Once such businesses had settled on a product, they put a huge effort into developing predictable, repeatable and efficient operations and processes—with everyone's main focus on the tasks they had to achieve each day. There is a problem today, however, with efficiency being the primary value driver of a business. Due to technological advances and globalisation, the world of employment has become commoditised. Efficiency is the norm, and as a result, its value has dropped significantly.

Automation today is extending far beyond the routine manual tasks performed by low-skilled workers. In the next five years, human and drone robots, as well as artificially intelligent software programmes, are predicted to eliminate 6% of jobs in the US. It's the white-collar, knowledge-based employees, such as lawyers and accountants, who are predicted to see the most change. Research has estimated that 39% of jobs in the legal sector could be automated in the next ten years. It's also predicted that accountants have a 95% chance of losing their jobs to automation at some point in the future. Today, when a business draws its primary value from repetitive work and old-fashioned notions of efficiency, it will find it increasingly hard to monetise that value.

Facing continuous disruption from globalisation and the internet, many large enterprises are now setting up divisions that adopt the practices of start-ups and accelerators. They're told to focus ondisruption and innovation rather than imitative competition; meeting customer needs rather than adding new product features or focusing on agility and speed rather than cost efficiency. Sadly, these divisions often fail because they're staffed by corporate employees who have the mindset and skillet of the businesses they've been raised within. I hope you're getting the message by now: there has never been a better time in history to be an entrepreneur. It's entrepreneurs who are blazing the trail for business today, leaving corporates in the dust through our responsiveness to the customers we serve.

How value is generated today

Instead of efficiency, value is created in businesses today through creativity and innovation. This involves inventing new ideas and coming up with new and different ways to use technology, products and processes. Value is developed through bringing new products or service improvements to the market, finding new solutions to customer problems, or new ways to sell and deliver existing services. That's great news for us. Never before has there been an opportunity to be so underqualified yet thrillingly inventive, have so much fun, and get paid handsomely for thinking differently. This is truly the era of people power.

Consider Uber, a cab company valued at $62 Billion (in 2019) without even owning a single one of its vehicles. Their business model has created what is called the ripple effect in the on-demand economy, reflecting that the market today (i.e. what customers want) matters far more than the physical product.

For a start-up to be as successful as Uber, the first question all entrepreneurs should ask themselves is: Who am I creating value for?

Uber declares its mission as, "Transportation to be as reliable as running water for everyone, in every city in the world." So Uber creates value for anyone who wants to go from Point A to Point B within a city. But so does every other taxi service, and when Uber started, this was a highly competitive and commoditised industry. Uber achieved success by constantly evolving its service offer through the customer feedback it received. When it began, its target customers were wealthy, young people being serviced through what goes by the name of Uber Black today—a high-end, luxury sedan or SUV that comes directly to the kerbside. It further expanded its offer by introducing dynamic pricing, which provided value to people who prioritise convenience over cost at peak times; for example, late at night and at the weekend. It introduced UberPool for cost-conscious customers who were willing to share rides. It provided UberXL (minivans and large SUVs) for those who wanted to travel in a group. And then it expanded its dynamic, customer-driven offer around the world into over 450 cities across 65 countries (2019). With 75 million users, 35 million drivers, and 84-87% of the "hailing market" in the USA, Uber is a massive success story built from its relentless focus on value.

Exchanging "value vouchers" for wealth

One of my favourite authors, entrepreneur and internet millionaire M. J. DeMarco, talks about the futility of chasing wealth, the concept of which is linked to those old-fashioned businesses built on efficiency. He says you should think instead about value vouchers, discovering what you can provide to your customers that they both want and need, and then giving it to them. Once you've established a great product or service offer, you can then scale it up and make your millions, but value has to be maintained all the way up what is called the supply chain to make sure customer experience is never compromised.

If you're executing what I think of as a tentacle business—which could be a franchise or network marketing model, for example—the octopus your tentacle connects to, or your parent company, has created the primary value and your job is to sell their products to your customers and service them well. You can still make a great living focusing on customer sales and satisfaction, but the greatest rewards of today's value-driven culture belong to the inventors who've identified a profitable niche, created products or services within it, and developed the distribution channels that you've bought into.

So, step one of my value-creation methodology for entrepreneurs is to research your business idea. If you're someone who struggles with ideas, consider either working within a system that someone else has created in the first instance or partnering with a person for whom these ideas flow effortlessly. Remember, there's a place for everyone in business. Entrepreneurs need a great team around them. Entrepreneurial value creation is a fluid and creative process that not everyone finds easy. Particularly if you're getting started after a corporate career, it can be helpful to bring your skills to others who are already in the flow.

Research is an important first step and needs to be done before you waste valuable time, effort and money launching into the market. Don't get hung up on the concept of originality, as practically everything has been done before. There's no need to get it perfect at this point either. Your only job is to see if you can do something better than your competition and in a more unique and differentiated way. Find out where others are getting it wrong and be clear about how they're getting it right, too.

Step two of my value-creation methodology is to test the market. In order to do this, you have to face up to your inner critic and put something out, no matter how imperfect it is. You'll refine it over time. Even if you fail at your first attempt, just getting something out there will have moved you closer to success. Wear your fails like a badge of honour and be proud to join the illustrious club of mega-successful entrepreneurs who also have failed business ventures to their name. It's all part of the game. Be bold and stop worrying about how others might judge you. Just do it, as Nike advises us!

Step three of my value-creation methodology is to establish feedback loops. This can be discouraging if you do not have a robust internal mindset, which is why a lot of entrepreneurs need specific assistance and support in this area. The feedback loop is your first wave of response to what you put out. Total silence? Has anyone noticed? Raise your profile or give it time. Haters? Interesting. You've ruffled some feathers. Got to be a reason why. Buyers? Wow, you're on the right track. Keep going. Make it a priority to engage with your customers or the people who take an interest in what you're doing. Ask them what they think and incorporate the feedback into your evolving business strategy.

Step four of my value-creation methodology is to refine and re-engage with your market. Make the feedback loop continuous. At this point, and because you're obsessed with value, it's all about getting it right for your customers. Ask for further feedback and pay attention to the answers. Let them direct you. Watch your sales metrics. Are your customers buying from you in increasing volumes? This is where you start the process of serious business development, deciding which markets you're entering into and in what way to capture the hearts and minds of your next-level target audience.

Step five of the value-creation methodology is to build distribution channels that deliver your products or services quickly and smoothly, leading to immense customer satisfaction and repeat business. Remember, this is an all-important part of value creation. In today's fast-paced, technology- and consumer-driven society, you can't afford to be sloppy in this respect. If you are, you'll lose out to your competition and your hard work and investment will be wasted.

Always keep value at the heart of your offer and your success will be assured.

CHAPTER THIRTEEN:
Love Your Competition

"If we can keep our competitors focused on us, while we focus on the customer, ultimately we'll turn out all right." Jeff Bezos, Founder and Chief Executive Officer of Amazon.com

When I ran my international television design company, opportunities to acquire prestigious contracts worth a million-plus came up a few times a year. We were privileged to win some of these. The same handful of companies were always invited to pitch. There were two of us in London, one in New York, one in L.A. and a couple of others who aspired to step up to the design 'premier league'.

One of my tasks as MD was to receive the inquiries and negotiate terms with the client. I'd persuade them to pay a pitch fee of several thousand pounds and to limit the rivals invited to a maximum of two or three if they really pushed it. Of course, we had to back this up by actually stepping away if they wouldn't agree to our terms, which wasn't that hard. Because if they weren't prepared to invest in us seriously throughout the pitch period, it was because they didn't value us and our time would be wasted.

Yachts in Cannes

At the international events we all gathered at, such as the Cannes Television Festival, we would see our competitors in person. The meetings would be frosty, to say the least. Instead of us getting together in these staggeringly gorgeous settings to discuss industry standards and how we could assist one other, we would glare at each other across the yachts and luxury hotel lobbies. My CEO told me to check out who our rivals were talking to and slip into position after they'd left so we could find out whether there were any conversations worth having, too. I found this stressful, painful and lonely. There we were in one of the most beautiful places in the world, representing teams of incredibly talented designers whose job it was to make a stunning and commercially impactful brand and creative work. You'd think it would be paradise, but instead of enjoying it, I was stuck in the mindset and behaviours of fear and scarcity. It isolated us from the valuable peer support and intelligence that could have helped us, both individually and collectively.

We were all operating at the highest levels in our businesses, but we were doing it without any mindset or leadership support, which was rare in our industry at the time. We fell back on what we thought was the safe way to behave, which was actually just our egos hijacking us. Our egos are our primitive inner beings. They have two missions: to defend us from certain harm and to validate our desire for approval. That's where the phrase pandering to someone's ego comes from. We now know that enlightened and self-aware people need to challenge their egos. Our egos haven't evolved from our history as primates when the most common cause of death was being eaten, so they're not able to distinguish between real and imagined fears or attribute a level of sophistication to assessing them. The feelings we have towards our rivals are often super intense for this reason. Without the ability to think about it rationally, our egos decide we're about to get eaten. This is a gale-force-ten threat, they tell us, that we need to react to in a gale-force-ten way.

Competition is opportunity

So it's our egos that make us see competition as a massive threat rather than as a source of opportunity in our thriving business landscape. Giving in to our egos leads to a winner-takes-all mentality, whereby people either ignore competition in the belief they're above it or try to eliminate it to become the dominant market player. This thinking is misguided because it takes you away from what should be your key focus: harvesting intelligence from your customers to make your business and life the very best they can be.

No business operates in a vacuum, so the winner-takes-all mentality makes us weak. It's na ve to think we can either succeed blindly or crush everyone who gets in our way. Our competitors are like the torchbearers of our journeys. They can show us where to go next and help us choose the best course of action at any given time. If your competitors are copying you, that's a great sign. As I often tell my children: Imitation is the sincerest form of flattery. You must be doing something right, so keep blazing a trail in your sector and getting noticed for the amazing things you're doing.

The world we live in thrives on competition and we all benefit as a result. Competition results in better products and services. It's good for consumers and good for business. It drives economic growth and increases standards of living. Competition through free trade is the basis of successful economies worldwide. When businesses compete with each other, customers get the best prices and quality of goods and services. Competition boosts innovation and causes the invention of new and better products, as well as more efficient processes. Many products that are commonplace today were once innovative breakthroughs. Cars, planes, phones, televisions, computers and many drugs and medicines all demonstrate how competition has the capacity to improve lives and increase prosperity.

Of course, it's inevitable that we're going to lose out to our competitors sometimes. Because of our egos, most of us truly hate that experience, but losing is a part of everyone's life and it's never going to be the end of you. Pick yourself up and tell yourself a bigger and better opportunity awaits on the other side. Tell yourself that God or the Universe, for a reason you may not understand right now, just decided it wasn't right for you to win at that time.

There's another purpose for loving your competition. Negative thoughts don't lead to positive results. When your brain focusses on your rivals and you allow feelings of jealousy, bitterness or fear to dominate, you stop focussing on yourself and what you can do better in life. Ask yourself where do you want to sit: in a place of darkness and bad-feeling or a place of freedom and light? As Martin Luther

King said, "Hatred paralyses life; love releases it. Hatred confuses life; love harmonises it. Hatred darkens life; love illuminates it."

Your rivals are not your enemies. Their main goal in life is not to hurt you. They're just trying to do something for themselves and their loved ones, like you, which is to make a great living and enjoy life along the way. They're solving the same problems as you. That means they're always thinking, always experimenting and always learning about the same things, too. You learn from their mistakes as they learn from yours. They expand your horizons as you expand theirs. They create a context within which your business exists. They help you identify trends and set benchmarks for comparing your performance. Only you and they know what it takes to walk this path, so whenever those unpleasant feelings of envy, insecurity and dislike come up, which they will because your ego is so powerful, say no to them firmly and thank your rivals instead. Ask for help appreciating the benefits they're bringing to you. Trust that everything is unfolding in the right way, for the right reason, and at that the right time for you to experience your very best life with their help along the way.

Humanise your competitors

One of the best ways to feel better about your competition is to humanise them, which means honouring your connection to them through your universal oneness or human experience. We all struggle and have challenges in life, and often the challenges we're experiencing are exactly the same as those of our rivals. "I don't like that man," said Abraham Lincoln once. "I must get to know him better." "Be kind, for everyone you meet is having a hard battle," said the ancient Egyptian philosopher Philo. Remember, even the most annoying people or the ones you perceive to be a direct or immediate threat may have been the victims of the worst mistreatment and the most emotional pain or deprivation. They may be fighting a heroic struggle against the odds simply to function in daily life. Who are you to add to their pain?

Our insecurities can be like a form of poverty; they make us mean and stop us from giving credit where credit is due. They also keep us from sensing the pain and fear our rivals sometimes experience and how much they might appreciate kind words or thoughts from us. So, rather than wishing pain, suffering or hardship on your rivals, wish them the best and set yourself free. Healthy competition is truly one of your greatest assets for growth. Its existence moves you towards excellence. It's also ongoing validation that a market actually exists for your products or services. So, instead of wanting your rivals to fail, see competition as a catalyst that helps you become great at what you do. You can only know how strong you are when faced with resistance and challenge, so embrace competition rather than resenting it. Transform envy into healthy motivation by appreciating your rivals and the freedom to be the best and most empowered version of you will result.

CHAPTER FOURTEEN:
How to Measure Performance

Put a system in place

Measuring performance is a task-based system that firmly sits under the umbrella of management as opposed to leadership. For restless, curious leaders, who are focussed on innovation, measuring performance can seem like an interminably dreary task, bogging you down in detail, spreadsheets, performance reviews, analysis and tracking. If the thought of this work sends shivers down your spine, remember that although the work does need to be done, it doesn't need to be done by you. Whether you hire in an HR consultant or advisor to set a system up for you or you employ someone as a manager and gatekeeper of this work, having these systems in place will make your life less chaotic and your business less stressful. This allows you, as its leader, the freedom to operate within your zone of genius or excellence.

I like to keep my insights clear and relatable, so I set myself a challenge to explain performance metrics in a way that is both easy to understand and easy for small business owners to apply. To do this, I'm going to look at two concepts, KRAs (key results areas) and KPIs (key performance indicators).

Key results areas

Let's start with KRAs. KRAs, or key results areas, can be applied to your business as a whole, or they can be applied to someone's performance at work. They're the things you absolutely have to do to make your business or position successful. In all job roles and businesses, there are only a few key results areas that matter so it can be relatively straightforward to define your own. The reason why KRAs are called key results areas is because they relate to the results you get rather than your activities. If your business is a marketing agency, for example, your core activities might involve designing websites, logos or ads, creating marketing strategies, or implementing media campaigns for clients. If you're the owner, your core activities might involve meeting new clients, attending and presenting at pitches for new business, and leading and directing your board or management team.

The KPIs, on the other hand, relate to the performance of these core activities. So they'll be focussed on tracking (for example) how profitable your projects are, how much repeat business you get from your clients, and the quality of that business. They can also track the results you are getting from your marketing activities; intelligence that can show you where and how to invest your money, as well as your efforts, for best results.

For example, when I first joined my design agency in London, a lot of the client inquiries revolved around low-value, ultra-competitive television title sequence work. This carried thin margins, and resulted in poor morale. I recognised that by positioning ourselves at a strategic corporate identity level, we could attract bigger contracts with less competition. That's exactly what happened, resulting in a full-forward leaping of profits over the course of eighteen months. This led to the business attracting the attention of and being sold to a major US communications group, Interpublic, for many multiples of that profit. It was all because of defining four key results areas, which were as follows: getting projects with a value exceeding £100k, getting paid for pitches that had a maximum of three other companies involved, getting international work, which commanded a premium, and getting work that was defined as corporate. In other words, work involving logo designs and associated rollout, which was the most profitable work because it was all produced in-house.

We also attached financial targets to each goal and the company as a whole. We were very clear about our break-even profit and growth metrics. Yes, it was as simple as that. And, it was the key to highly paid and happy staff, healthy dividends, and ultimately a big payout for me, as one of the shareholders in the business.

Key results areas are clear and tangible. They don't depend on third parties and can't be delegated. I couldn't have set a KRA in the design business linked to: 'clients bringing more interesting work to our company'. As what a designer defined as interesting might not be what I thought was interesting. Besides, I had no control over the clients' choices and decisions to bring us that work. However, it was certainly possible, through our clearly defined KRAs, to put ourselves in a prime position to receive the right inquiries, and smash the competition, through our innovative ideas and exciting designs.

When you hire someone, having KRAs in place will make them clear about the reason you took them on, as well as telling you both whether they're doing their job in the best possible way. KRAs focus attention on the results that you expect of someone rather than their day-to-day activities. It helps them understand the most critical tasks and what they must do to achieve them. When you give people a detailed description of their job function with a clear expectation of performance, you allow them to focus on getting the results you need from them.

The Pareto principle, otherwise known as the 80/20 rule, is a popular concept in business, although, it also applies to life in general. It states that the majority of results—call it 80%, although, it's not always as exact a figure as this—comes from the minority of inputs, the 20%. 20% of your customers contribute 80% of your revenue. 20% of your sales team create 80% of your sales. 20% of the most reported software bugs cause 80% of software crashes. 20% of your time produces 80% of your results. It's important to know this as it underlines the importance of KRAs and prevents everyone from wasting time on the wrong activities. When setting KRAs, always ask yourself and others, what 20% of your work drives 80% of your outcomes?

Key performance indicators

KPIs, or key performance indicators, differ from KRAs in that they start with a set of goals or objectives against which progress is tracked and reported. They're used to evaluate the success of a business or its activities, and also to compare a company against others in the same sector. The effect of having KPIs in place is that it lets you see whether and by how much your business is succeeding against your stated goals. One of your business goals, for example, might be to take a 20% increase in market share against your main competitor. Your main KPI or performance indicator may, therefore, be the measure of your turnover compared to theirs. Or, you could set your goal as a 20% increase in profits this year. You would clearly be able to see from your accounts whether this has been achieved.

Key performance indicators are mostly focussed on things like revenue and profit margins. But, since business success depends on other things too, they can also focus on factors like customer satisfaction, employee turnover, repeat versus new business, client acquisition and operational efficiency. KPIs are only as useful as the action they inspire. If you set unrealistic goals for your business, you probably won't create the positive change you're looking for, so always base them around goals that are SMART. SMART standing for: specific, measurable, achievable, relevant and time-bound.

You can use your KPIs in conjunction with KRAs. Let's say you've taken on a business development person to serve your goal of expanding your business in a new and promising sector. You can set them a KRA, for example, of getting new income-generating clients to produce revenues of 300k within six months. The weekly KPIs that might accompany this could be, for example, attending two networking events, having two face-to-face meetings and four telephone conversations, creating one speaker opportunity and having ten new conversations per week on social media.

You can also use KPIs to motivate you to achieve your personal goals. For example, when writing this book, I set myself the goal of three chapters a week, minimum, and I made sure I stuck to this no matter what. When you're setting a KPI, it's useful to ask yourself questions such as, what is the desired outcome? Why does it matter? How will I measure progress? How can I influence it? Is it me or someone else who is responsible? How will we know we've achieved the right outcome? Also, decide when and how often you're going to review progress, as there is not much point in setting KPIs if you don't use them. The best KPIs don't require huge shifts to achieve. They focus, rather, on easy-to-achieve steps that keep you on track for your goal.

There are several good CRM (customer relationship management) software apps or tools that allow you to track KPIs. If your business is growing and has departments and employees to manage, it is a good idea to investigate these. I wish you every success with your KRAs and KPIs. Use them to keep yourself and everyone else on track for your goals.

CHAPTER FIFTEEN:
A Fair Exchange

In its most basic form, the concept of a fair exchange is easy to understand. It's about an exchange of value that works for both parties. Think of the good feeling you get when you buy what you consider to be a bargain. For a transaction to happen, value has to be created for the other side, too. Maybe the bargain is there because the seller has excess stock that they need to get rid of. Maybe their product hasn't sold as well as they hoped. Maybe they dropped their price to expand their market share. A fair exchange is the first principle of trading, and it's been around for centuries. We'll look at a fair exchange in business shortly, but first I'd like to look at how the concept of a fair exchange can become confused in relationships. This is when this simple transactional concept gets mixed up with people's values.

The role of values

Unlike the things you've bought, our unique experience of life means we bring different values to our concept of what matters most. Many of us make the mistake of believing there are absolute truths in this respect, but there aren't. Our views are just thoughts and opinions shaped by our own experience. They're stories we tell ourselves to justify our actions. Let's use the example of a stay-at-home wife who cooks, cleans and looks after the children while her husband goes to work. She believes she makes an equal contribution to the family as her husband. Whether this view is shared or not by him depends on his values. If he appreciates being relieved of dull domestic chores in order to focus on his work and believes that his wife is performing the unique and valuable role of bringing up their children, then he appreciates her equally and their marriage is good. You could say they share their values in this respect.

Her husband might not feel this way, though. Or perhaps he once did but doesn't any more. If he's under pressure financially, his highest might values shift. Rather than appreciating his wife relieving him of the burden of domestic and childcare work, he might start to resent her lack of financial contribution. He might want her to work outside the home, which again is fine, as long as he realises that, as a consequence, more demands will be placed upon him. Perhaps he'll have to give up the luxury of being looked after and having a home-cooked meal prepared for him each night. Or maybe she'll ask him to look after the children while she pursues independent interests or a social life. That's what a fair exchange looks like in healthy relationships.

When the concept of a fair exchange goes wrong between people, they judge the actions of the other person by their own values. They discount the perspective of the other partner and allow theirs to dominate. Let's revert to our husband and stay-at-home wife. Perhaps she's found herself some employment but is still doing all the childcare and domestic work. In her mind, she's increased her contribution and deserves a reward for that. Perhaps the husband is still supporting his family 100% while his wife spends her newfound earnings on luxuries for herself and the children. He asks her to pay the bills instead, which upsets her. Both parties start to feel dissatisfied and both believe they're on the receiving end of an unfair exchange. Without understanding the concept of differing values, people only judge what's fair and reasonable according to their own.

When the wife bought luxuries, she thought her husband would be pleased to see her exercising some financial independence. She also thought he'd appreciate that she and the children were better dressed without it having to be funded by him. This thinking came from her own values, which she transferred unquestioningly to him. The husband, on the other hand, with his top value of financial security, was looking forward to more money in the bank, especially since there'd been some redundancies at work and he was feeling insecure about his ability to take care of his family. He thought his wife and children were perfectly attractive just the way they were, and those expensive shoes she spent her money on didn't make him feel any better about her. This thinking also came from his own values, which he expected her to prioritise. Before long, our husband and wife aren't talking. Their marriage is under strain. Accusations fly, and each of them feels unappreciated and unsupported. Each one feels locked into an unfair exchange. Resentment creeps in and love flies out the door. Sound familiar? These types of scenarios, or versions of them, arise all the time between soon-to-be-divorced couples.

So what's the solution to a fair exchange between people and how could our troubled husband and wife have achieved it? The answer is an understanding of one another's values. For every key relationship in your life, whether in business or your personal life, it's important both to understand what matters most to the other person, and to demonstrate that understanding through your communications and behaviour. Recognise that someone else's values will always be different to your own, and a fair exchange means recognising and balancing both. You can't be loving to someone—or be a great business partner, salesperson, employee or boss—unless you take the time to find out and consistently address what other people truly care about. Stay curious. Ask the right questions—and keep asking as people's values change over time. If you put in the effort to do this, your relationship with others should transform for the better. And if they don't, the other person may not be the right long-term match for you.

Consequences of an unfair exchange

Let's look more closely at a fair exchange in business. As already discussed, a fair exchange is, at its most basic, a transactional issue about buying or selling a product or service. With simple, low-cost purchases, most of us feel only mild annoyance if we think value has not been provided by the product or service we have bought. This is because we can limit the value we give in return in the form of not making repeat purchases or giving a poor review and not recommending the product or service to others. However, it's not uncommon for people to absorb losses that may have personally cost them thousands or even tens of thousands of pounds. When this is the case, we can feel huge bitterness and even hatred towards the people we believe have ripped us off or created what feels like a massively unfair exchange of value.

As human beings, one of the worst experiences we can have in life is being taken advantage of by others at our own expense. We, and most mammals, are social species, so we're biologically programmed to expect fairness. Living and working in communities, as we do, requires us to put our trust in others. If this trust is betrayed, it can strike at the very heart of our belief in ourselves. I have experienced this myself since I invested (and lost) a lot of money with a highly unethical developer who protected himself very carefully on a development project whilst exposing his investors to 100% of the risk. It hurt, a lot.

It's unrealistic to expect anyone to bounce back quickly from this type of betrayal, but it can be helpful to know that serious financial loss and fraud are common. A lot of people don't reveal their mistakes in this respect to others as they can provoke a feeling of intense shame and embarrassment, which is, of course, what their perpetrators rely on. It's rarely possible to emerge from significant financial loss feeling strong and ready to take on the world, but you can both protect yourself and choose a gentle path to recovery that transfers accountability to the person who created your pain. I go into this in more depth in my second book.

So how can we protect ourselves from those who seek to help themselves to our value without creating value for us in return? And how can we build relationships that powerfully support us as a result of the fair exchange that's created?

Principles of a fair exchange in business

Here are my five principles for establishing a fair exchange:

1. Communicate your offer and your expectations clearly.

One of the worst things you can do in business as well as life is to make promises that you don't keep. When you do this, everyone suffers, including you. So, make sure everyone you deal with knows and understands what you have committed to, as well as what you need from others to make this happen. Check with the other party as to whether this feels fair and reasonable. If things change, and you're no longer able to meet your original commitments, always acknowledge this fully and start afresh in making new ones. Clarity builds value.

2. Ask questions and keep assumptions low.

This is not the same as adopting a cynical or suspicious attitude towards others. We all know people like this, and they're very hard to be around. What this means is that instead of deciding everyone and everything is going to be just fine, stay alert to potential problems. Always check someone else's expectations and decide whether you can realistically deliver on them. Also ask whether they can realistically deliver on yours. It's amazing how many people fail to do this.

3. Insist on a written agreement for any business arrangement that involves you investing time, effort or money.

Any business relationship that involves committing a significant amount of either time or money should be accompanied by a written agreement that defines where each party thinks they're creating value. Does the other party recognise this as value too—in other words, are your values shared? Of course, it's easier if they are, but many times, if people are transparent, this will not be the case, so a carefully negotiated compromise is required. This is why I like formal written agreements. It makes the shared understanding of created value concrete and tangible, which is reassuring to all concerned.

4. Read the fine print carefully and don't accept things at face value.

The devil is in the detail. Take great care to read and fully understand the fine print in any contract or written agreement. Don't sign anything that you don't understand. Lawyers are experts at inserting clauses in otherwise innocuous documents that could topple you if you're not careful. This is exactly how I got ripped off. Investing in great lawyers to double check any agreement you're being asked to sign is always worthwhile, especially where large sums of money are involved.

5. Look to negotiate, compromise and find common ground.

   A fair exchange of value is about evolving healthy, win-win relationships. All relationships are dynamic and change constantly. So, whatever you agree at the outset, make sure you revisit the terms periodically to see whether your understanding and expectations have altered. And if they have, be flexible and accommodate yours and the other party's perspective and wishes. Never force outcomes on other people, as such manipulative behaviour is a clear sign of an unequal exchange of value. Relationships will always fail if one party insists on dominating at the expense of the other.

There will always be people in life who will try to help themselves to the value you provide, monetary or otherwise, without giving anything in return. Protect yourself from them by adopting these principles—and make a fair exchange a principle that you abide by always.

CHAPTER SIXTEEN:
Build a Wealthy Network

"The richest people in the world build networks, everyone else is trained to look for work."

Robert Kiyosaki.

Wealthy people are just people

When I trained in professional property investment, I was told it's important to find investors to fund the equity portion of your property deals. This is because unless you're also a high-net-worth individual or a developer with many deals you've already exited profitably, the funds for your projects will quickly run out, leaving you stuck and unable to grow your business. When I first heard this, the advice that was given alongside it was to find rich people by going to the places they hang out, such as flying clubs, elite networking events and charity balls. But after following this advice and having had several frustrating encounters with the wealthy people I met there, I formed a much saner conclusion, which is that you should definitely not aim to hang out with rich people. Because rich people are just people. Good, bad and indifferent. Clueless and selfish. Kind or mean spirited. Arrogant know-it-alls or curious and open. You should always apply the same high standards to wealthy people that you would to all your friends and business associates. Only then will you find your gold.

It's a bit like dating. If you're an attractive female, and you post pics on a dating site that show off your gym-honed body in a thong bikini, you'd be inundated with potential dates. But many of these guys would be the type you'd actively try to avoid if they cornered you at a party. Whereas if you posted a more low-key set of pics, wearing everyday clothes and saying you're looking for a serious relationship, you'd get fewer likes. But you'd know the guys who swiped right were more likely to be sincere, rather than players who just want to use you. Employ a similar tactic with rich people. Stay true to you rather than trying hard to please. Some of the wealthy people you meet may be too entitled and puffed up with arrogance to think anything you say or do, as a poorer person, will be of value to them. But that doesn't mean there aren't some great wealthy people out there who are open to meeting someone just like you. You just have to maintain your standards when looking for them, and step away from others who fall short.

Why entrepreneurs need a wealthy network

Your business may be completely unconnected to property, so you may be wondering what the value of a wealthy network could be to you? A wealthy network is another way of saying successful people. The right wealthy people are those you can learn from and leverage to make your life and business successful. There is no obligation on you to find or network with people like this, but it is helpful if you are taking your business to the next level, to be around people who have done this already and are willing to share their wisdom and experience with you. Like many entrepreneurs, I've invested heavily in education, masterminds and mentors myself, but I also have to say: why waste your money on courses if you have go-to people in your network who will answer any question you put to them based on their extensive, real-world experience of success? This is the true value of a wealthy network. Such people often really enjoy encouraging and guiding younger or less-experienced entrepreneurs, so don't think they're only doing you a favour!

Perhaps you've heard the quote, "Your network is your net worth?" Or if you haven't, perhaps you've heard another, by the motivational speaker Jim Rohn, who said, "You're the average of the five people you spend the most time with?" I don't think these words of wisdom are telling us to ditch our poorer friends and family members and only hang out with wealthy people instead. Of course, it's great to have successful people to turn to for advice, support and money for our business or projects, but value in any relationship has to work for both parties. If you're poor in monetary terms and looking for either wealthy mentors or cash-rich investors, there's certainly plenty you can offer them. Opportunities, expertise, time, integrity, effort, humour, availability, charm, market insights, good company and great conversation—the list is endless. But they have to value what you're offering for it to work. If all they care about is money and you don't have it, guess what? No matter how much you're offering to them, the door will be closed in your face. Many wealthy people, because they're just people like the rest of us, are empty and afraid. In fact, sometimes they're rich simply because they haven't been able to find a better way to deal with their pain. And empty and afraid people have nothing to offer you, no matter what their net worth or status is in life.

If you have a goal of becoming wealthy yourself, you should always care more about the value you're creating for others rather than the wealth itself, which is an inevitable by-product of value. So, as well as asking yourself how you can create value for others, you also need to ask yourself, what are you really chasing? The supercars and designer handbags are toys; they're nice to have but no substitute for a meaningful life and the close intimate relationships we all crave. When you're struggling, you may ache at times to have the luxuries you don't have to think twice about buying, but even an endless supply won't make you happy if you haven't learned how to use our wealth for its true purpose, which is to create freedom, time and love in your life.

A massive gift of wealth is that it enables people to show love to many more than they could touch individually. Some of the wealthiest entrepreneurs in the world are also the most generous, since they started out with an intention to create value for millions. After they'd done this, they then found happiness through donating a large chunk of their fortune to charity. Billionaires such as Bill Gates and Warren Buffett are huge philanthropists. They achieve joy and peace through giving. So I truly support your success, and I wish you all the wealth you desire because, since you're still reading, I get the feeling you'll be someone who'll also use yours to make a difference in the world.

Let's revisit our two quotes in light of this. "Your network is your net worth," and "You're the average of the five people you spend the most time with." If you agree with my premise that the ultimate goal of wealth is to create a life filled with love and freedom, your network should evolve to reflect this. As with everything you do, you need to start with the end in mind. Cultivate relationships with like-minded people who possess a generosity of spirit and are using their wealth to make their world a more loving place. If you don't already move in circles that give you physical access to such people, you'll usually be able to receive their knowledge and wisdom cheaply or even for free through books, education and social media. Improve yourself continuously, learn to think the way they do, and when the time is right and the opportunity arises, you'll be in the right place to build these real-world connections.

Believe you're worth it

Never tell yourself someone like you can't move in these exalted circles. We don't need a whole roomful of successful, connected people to be our friends. Like a husband or wife, we only need one to make a big difference to us. Be patient. Someone who is the right kind of person to take you to the next level will have friends who are similar to them. The right type of person will probably not have set out to build wealth alone, as these types of people, as discussed, only value people who are rich too. Rather, they probably set out to build an exciting business or life that made a difference to many and therefore generated wealth for them as its creator. For someone like this, it's the quality of every relationship that counts. Be clear about the value you can bring to them. How can you help this person fulfil their higher purpose? How can you demonstrate that you're someone with next-level integrity too? Remember: to attract a certain type of person to you, you have to be that person first.

So to summarise: Don't waste time on rich people whose values are based on accumulating wealth alone. Unless these people truly prioritise relationships, goals and commitments outside their work and immediate family, the door will always be closed to you. Let them pass through your life, but don't try to make them part of it. They won't have anything to give you. You will exist for one reason alone: to make them richer so they can buy more toys for themselves and their family. Remember that rich people are just people—good, bad and indifferent. Keep your standards high, and when anyone shows you disrespect or an attitude of superiority, set them free.

If you're into the concept of wealth creation and business success, you should realise that not everyone who has something to offer you will have money. However much of a priority it is to us, wealth creation is not part of everyone's value system. Remember, we still need a powerful home team. Lots of people don't have much materially, but they still belong in your home team if they have abundance in a different area of their lives. If they have the three Ps—passion, purpose and positivity—we should let their attitude and spirit inspire us. Let them remind us that, whether we're rich, poor or in between, we can always be the best version of ourselves. Remember, the best things in life are the people we love, the places we've been and the memories we've made along the way. Never settle for second best when it comes to relationships.

CHAPTER SEVENTEEN:
The Real Win-win

I was introduced to the concept of win-win, which is particularly popular in property circles, when I read the bestselling business and performance book, The 7 Habits of Highly Effective People by Stephen Covey. Covey explains that in every decision we make, we must plan for others to benefit from our actions too. This is harder to achieve than you might think. Most of us are actually programmed by ancient fear and a mindset of scarcity to take the opposite path, which means we often try to win at the expense of others. Personally, I have seen many times over that win-win is the elite law of human connection and business success, whilst win-lose inevitably results in personal as well as business loss.

Understand what winning looks like for others

Win-win behaviour comes from the ability to work with the perspective and wishes of others. If you're approaching a situation with a win-win attitude, you'll understand what winning looks like for the other person and you'll believe there are lasting benefits for both of you in adopting this approach. You won't be pushing for something the other person doesn't want and you won't feel pushed into doing something that you're uncomfortable with. When you're in win-win mode, you'll be treated with respect, and you'll be treating the other party respectfully, too. You'll be brainstorming outcomes that work for everyone, rather than having them dictated to you. You won't be disrespected or shut down for evolving your thinking or changing your mind.

If, like many people, you're someone who finds it hard to trust others, being in the open and collaborative space of win-win may feel deeply uncomfortable for you. You'll probably experience it as a loss of control or power. You'll feel fear, too, because this is unfamiliar territory for you. Give it time. Commit to win-win as a habit, allow your discomfort to come up, and keep going. Eventually, people will associate this approach with you and they'll be more likely to respond in the same way. If they don't, just remember that bullies, or victims of bullies, are heavily invested in the drama of win-lose. If you're someone who's trying to engage with another person in a win-win way and they shut you down, it's because they don't want to give up their win-lose power play. This is a toxic situation for you.

Win-win isn't something you'll be able to perfect immediately. In fact, your understanding and use of it will be linked to your attitude towards yourself and your levels of self-awareness, as well as your determination to live a great life free of relationship conflict. Because win-win exists within the panoply of inspiring behaviours that people who are powerfully committed to becoming the best versions of themselves adopt, it's a synergistic concept. I know some people in property who believe they always adopt win-win principles, but, in fact, they use the concept as a manipulative tool to negotiate deals that are massively weighted in their favour. Win-win is never about manipulating people or about using education and intelligence to con them out of something that is rightfully theirs. I'm sure you know the difference.

Let's look at how the perfect law of win-win manifests elsewhere in life. Although some people think win-lose is at the heart of competitive sport, sport is actually a great example of win-win. Watching and participating in sport is a very pleasurable activity for many people. Winning or losing is the inevitable outcome of competing; it's what makes it exciting, but losing at sport is just part of the game. The rules are clear from the outset. Losing at sport is simply a consequence of participating. And being a good loser shows that you have a team spirit and are able to celebrate others' successes as well as your own. So, although in sport there are technically losers as well as winners, there's a massive win-win of enjoyment for all concerned.

You may also think of wealth as a win-lose scenario in our capitalist society. In this context, wealth might not look at all like fun unless you're the person that has it. Not everyone can be wealthy or have everything they want in life. In fact, as we all know, most people in the world struggle to put food on the table. To turn wealth from win-lose into a win-win scenario means wealthy people have to use their wealth in turn to improve the lives of others, and that's exactly what many big-hearted philanthropists love to do. So, wealth, when used wisely, also results in a massive win-win for all. As Nelson Mandela said, "There can be no greater gift than helping others without expecting anything in return."

What win-win looks like in business

How about business? The most market-driven and entrepreneurial companies will always win the most customers, leaving their rivals struggling, but embedded within this is also a win-win outcome that works perfectly for the customer and the company they buy from. If your product or service doesn't compete, it's because you're not meeting your customers' needs or someone else is meeting them better. So here, too, the law of win-win rewards those who create value for others and penalises those who don't.

Many entrepreneurs struggle to find their ideal client and price their product or service offerings at the right level to achieve a win-win outcome. Pricing tends to be more straightforward and can be calculated by factoring in your production and human resource costs, as well as the profit you need to stay in business. To find your ideal customer, it's helpful to follow their patterns of interest—read what they read, watch what they watch, post comments, pictures and videos on forums they subscribe to and get high-profile speaking engagements at events they attend. If you're in a service business, message your prospects on social media and set up introductory calls to ascertain their needs. You should also network personally at their industry events, trade shows and conferences. This is how you begin to understand what it looks like for them to win. And this is also how they start to believe their concerns, worries, fears and problems could be solved by you. After a while, they'll even forget that it's YOU who built the relationship. You've become one of them—a person they see as a trusted member of their inner circle. That's business development perfection.

All this is an important precursor to them understanding that you are the potential purveyor of a win-win scenario. You have to EARN this right in the first instance by putting in the effort and showing up in the right way. It is a dead giveaway of a win-lose attitude if you turn up and immediately demand attention or respect without putting in this preliminary effort.

I recently attended a network marketing event in London that a friend of mine, who was involved in the business, invited me to. I attended this event with another friend who happened to be a successful board director of a major construction company. We'd decided to go to the event, which was ostensibly about "improving our energy levels" to support my (girl)friend and have dinner afterwards, so I informed her in advance we could only join the event for 90 minutes. She said that was fine as the meeting was only scheduled to last an hour or so. We sat through her short presentation, which was low-key and interesting. She weaved anecdotes about her life and personal journey into information about the supplements she was promoting and introduced her husband who shared his personal experience and a few jokes too. They created value for the audience by keeping their presentation short, authentic and fun. Prior to this, she'd also created a lot of value for me in various ways, so I was very happy to support her in turn. I also knew I'd be expected to purchase a few supplements and I'd already decided that was ok.

After my friend's short presentation a man leapt up and delivered a long presentation on the company itself, eagerly presenting the network marketing model and the fantastic "opportunity" to earn money by becoming a promoter of their supplements too. He barely paused for breath; his presentation was long and "salesy". After a great start to the evening, this took my friend and me by surprise. We hadn't expected to be pitched to so heavily – especially not for half an hour or more. It was a little uncomfortable, and we left early.

The presenter made the incorrect assumption that the audience was composed of people keen to consider their sales-based supplementary income stream.

He didn't take time beforehand to mingle, ask us questions or to find out who we were and why we had come to the event. He didn't deliver prior value; he hadn't earned the right to pitch. It was a shame, as I'm sure he was a very nice man. But he misunderstood the win/win law of successful salesmanship, just as my friend understood it. I don't know how many sales he made that night, but I can understand why she's the one that keeps winning those holidays to Las Vegas and he's wearing an ill-fitting grey suit and scuffed shoes. LOL.

Five ways to build win-win outcomes with others

Here are five ways you can build win-win relationships with your prospects and clients.

1. Ask them about their vision and mission. What do they want to accomplish? How do they define success?

2. Who do they serve and what matters to their customers?

3. How can you help them to either reach or exceed their goals?

4. Where do they feel they've had success in the past?

5. Are they open to new ways of communicating with and servicing their customers?

In asking these questions, you create a climate of open communication and position yourself as a valued resource who is truly committed to their success.

I hope you're beginning to see that win-win results in a happy outcome for every situation. It's a universal law that builds connection and satisfaction. Recognise and accept this truth. You never have to accept win-lose or believe it's the right outcome—ever.

CHAPTER EIGHTEEN:
Your Business Story

We humans are hardwired to respond to stories. It's in our DNA. We only have to look back to the era of cave paintings to recognise that our capacity to tell stories is one of the key things that differentiates us humans from our animal counterparts. Stories affect your brain in ways that facts never do. They inspire powerful emotion. They build connection and create engagement. They help others to trust and obtain meaning and enjoyment from their experience of you. Stories strengthen personal connections, and in business, they help your customers and employees believe they can make a difference to the world and the people they serve.

Your empowered personal story

We all create personal stories for ourselves that are based not on facts but on an emotional narrative with us as the lead actor. Repetition of this story with your personal spin on it can cause you to view yourself in many different ways: a victim, a hero, an amazing friend or family member, an action taker or a coward. Regardless of the voices that were installed in your head as a child or your difficult early experiences, it's never too late to revisit your personal story and recognise the lessons and benefits that accompanied the journey you've had in life. This doesn't mean you should rewrite the facts, as the facts are what they are, and to rewrite them. That's commonly known as denial, and it makes you lose integrity and damages your connection with others. Rather, it's taking the opportunity to view your life exactly as it is, but through a more grateful, forgiving and empowered lens.

It's important to mention this because the first step to telling a great business story is to have a powerful personal story that you're willing to share with others. This is at the heart of your personal brand. People don't resonate emotionally with those who hide their challenges and struggles and pretend their life's one big picnic. They seem too closed, impersonal and distant. They create bad feelings such as jealousy and distrust in others. It is far more powerful to be open about your struggles and challenges and show how you've emerged better and stronger out the other side. Everyone loves a survivor, so use your struggles, setbacks and bounce backs to inspire others to be better and more empowered versions of themselves too.

Separate purpose from profit

When it comes to business, especially if you're an entrepreneur, you also have a story to tell. Of course, your company is out to make a profit and win a decent share of your market, but it exists for other reasons too. You could have chosen to get into any business in any industry, but there's a reason you made the choice in business you did. This reason is your story. It's what's going to attract customers to you and build engagement with your stakeholders. Having a business story is part of your leadership role. It serves to inspire your employees as well as your customers. It embodies a wider purpose in relation to you as well as others.

Let's look at some brands and companies that have a great strapline and story. Apple wants us to "think different". Harley Davidson wants us to "have more exciting lives". Nike wants us to "just do it" and live our lives with a spirit of limitless adventure. Ben and Jerry's wants "happy cows, happy farmers, a happy planet". Heineken "refreshes the parts other beers can't reach". L'Or al wants us to believe "we're worth it". Skittles wants us to "taste the rainbow."

GoPro, Inc., which commands us to "Think it. See it. Do it", is an American technology company that manufactures action cameras and develops its own mobile apps and video-editing software. The name came about as the founder, Nick Woodman, and his surfing friends all aspired to become professional surfers. "Going Pro" was both their ultimate goal, and the only way they could be filmed on the water before they developed their cameras. What started with a 35MM camera and a wrist strap made from old wetsuits and plastic scraps has today grown into an international company that has sold over 26 million GoPro cameras in over 100 countries. What began as a simple idea to help athletes document themselves in action has today become a standard for how people capture themselves engaged in their interests, whatever they may be. GoPro's story is that it "helps people capture and share their lives' most meaningful experiences".

The Weight Watchers brand is about people making healthier choices in life, looking slimmer and feeling better about themselves. But the company took it further with an amazing business story, promoted through its "Awaken Your Incredible" campaign. This story connects emotionally with the underlying reason people want to lose weight—to become be the very best version of themselves; the person within that got lost along the way. It works because they found a way to make their brand less about a product and more about a feeling. That's an example of a great business story, too.

When businesses and brands think of themselves in this way, we don't think of them as selling to us. We think of them as helping us. Strictly speaking, these statements define their core purpose rather than story, but behind every purpose lies a story, so the purpose or reason why for your company's existence comes first.

How to "start with why"

In his book Start With Why: How Great Leaders Inspire Action, author Simon Sinek explored the difference between the market-leading Apples of the world and the also-ran competition and found that it starts with their why. To explain this concept, he refers to what he calls "the golden circle". The reason why is the centre or core belief of the business; it's why it exists. Next comes the how, which is how the business fulfils that core belief. And finally, it cascades down to what the company actually does.

What Sinek found is that most companies do their marketing backwards. They start with their what, and then move to the how. Most of these companies don't even think about the why. In fact, most of them don't even know why they do what they do. Sinek has found having loyal customers is all about attracting the people who share your beliefs. He found that people don't buy what you do; they buy why you do it. This might seem obvious, but it's a step that's most often overlooked. If you were or are the founder of your business, wouldn't you want the people marketing it to know why you started it in the first place? Understanding your why is essential to knowing how to communicate the how and the what.

Let's ask with starting you what your reason why is for your business. I'm going to tell you mine. My reason why (for my content-creation business) is to empower and inspire entrepreneurs to be the most successful and interpersonally connected versions of themselves. It can be summarised by the statement: "Connect with the best in you." Next, ask yourself how you do this. How I do this is by giving insights, encouragement and strategies to help entrepreneurs strengthen their relationships with the key people in their businesses and lives, including the most important connection of all, the ones they have with themselves.

Then what do you do to fulfil this? What I do is build an information bank of resources that are accessible to all and offer individual and group mentoring to bring sophistication, guidance and emotional intelligence to entrepreneurs who want to bring success and happiness to their relationships in business and life.

If we go back to your why and dig a bit deeper, you'll find your story. Here's mine. After a childhood spent witnessing the painful isolation and disconnection that characterised my parents' lives, I also spent what most people would consider a very successful and high-level career feeling unsupported, isolated, and vulnerable to people who ruthlessly prioritised their own agendas over mine. No one had modelled the value of authentic connection for me, and as a result, I had no idea how to seek it. Although I was trained and developed to professionally manage and profit from high-level relationships in business, which basically meant trained to perform like a seal for someone else, I had not been taught how to either communicate or achieve the results I wanted or needed for myself. My long, hard experiences, difficulties and struggles resulted in the wisdom and experience I am sharing with you today. And what a joy it is to be able to offer this.

So I created powerful tools and strategies, the ones I wish I'd had myself, which can transform entrepreneurs' relationships into ones that support their happiness and success. Now it's your turn. Have fun with your story. Think about the reason you founded your business before going deeper and connecting with that powerful emotional experience that others will resonate with. That's your magic—your gold, if you like—that will elevate you above your competitors and create true loyalty.

CHAPTER NINETEEN:
Business Partner Success

Why we partner in business

I've had several business partners in my career as I love working with other people. I have also been fortunate to have the benefit of watching many other business partnerships both succeed and fail. And in this chapter, I'm going to share with you some of the lessons I've learned. People seek business partners for many reasons. The first is the same reason we seek life partners: companionship. We're social creatures, and life is more fun if we're on our journey together. If we have someone to share the good and the bad times with. Someone to celebrate and commiserate with. Someone to bring a fresh perspective on things. Someone who's got skin in the game, too.

Business partnerships can be either a source of mutual benefit and joy or they can be a source of incredible stress, pain and hardship. The lessons in this chapter will help you avoid the wrong business partners and choose the right ones for sustained growth and success.

Your perfect business partner

Aside from the emotional benefit, another reason people establish partnerships is for leverage. Someone who does what you hate and actually enjoys it. Someone who has the experience, contacts or skills you don't. Someone who lets you concentrate on what you do best so that you can do more of it. Having different skill sets and interests to your business partner also frees you up to own your part of the business fully. This eliminates a lot of frustration and conflict down the line. People are drawn to others similar to themselves socially, but people just like you are not going to be your ideal business partner. If you're visionary and creative, you'll need a do-er to back you up. If you're big picture, you'll need somebody who's great with detail, and so on. It might take longer to establish a bond with people who are different from you, but they'll be your business gems. Over and above their complementary skill sets, look for congruent values and the willingness to tackle difficult issues openly and with integrity. Just like a marriage, when business partnerships go wrong, they go horribly wrong. Failing business partnerships cause failing businesses. There can be fights about money, about time and effort, about strategic direction, about lifestyle and other business interests. And while this is happening, entrepreneurial spirit and innovation get crushed. Business meltdown is the inevitable result.

Five principles for business partner success

I want you to have amazingly powerful and successful partnerships, so here are my five proven principles for business partner success:

1. **Have a great business history together.** A business partnership is like a marriage. It's a serious commitment, so no matter how much you like someone, don't jump in feet first. Get to know your prospective partner by working with them on one or more projects for at least a few months— preferably for a year or more—before you move on to a deeper relationship. Think of it like business dating before business engagement and finally business marriage. Working together on projects will help you become aware of areas of potential incompatibility and discord. If you think you've found someone promising to work with, but you don't have a common project and don't know them that well, move things forward by investing significant time with them. This should involve full days and even overnight stays on at least six different occasions rather than just having a phone

chat and/or coffee every couple of weeks. The purpose of these meetings should be to explore your goals, values and potential business arrangements together. It's better to fall out before you make any major and hard-to-reverse commitments—and investing a proper chunk of time is the best way to do this.

2. **Don't mix business and personal relationships.** Partnering with people you're in a romantic or personal relationship with is high risk unless you're deliberately creating a family business. And family businesses have different rules. Mixing business with pleasure introduces complexity, as the breakdown of personal relationships can negatively impact your business, too. What attracted you to someone personally is not the same as them having complementary skill sets and business experience. It makes it difficult to hire or engage other high-level people in your company, too, as they'll fear being marginalised by side conversations or pillow talk. This is also the reason nepotism is disliked by investors.

On many occasions, I've seen it go one of two ways with couples who work together. They either become effective business partners and their relationship starts to function on a purely practical rather than an emotional level, or they struggle with incompatible values and business experience, which then spills over into their romantic life. What a shame. Your life partner should be a support for you when times are tough, rather than stuck in the trenches with you. So, get clear on whether you want someone to be your business or life partner and act accordingly.

3. **Keep it simple.** All relationships are complex, and business relationships more complex than personal ones. This is because they involve one of the issues people squabble about most: money. If you assemble a team of six board directors who don't know one another and they haven't got a proven history of working successfully together, disaster will likely ensue. This is like a business version of polygamy, where a dominant partner forces additional "wives"—or in

this case, business partners—onto existing ones and just expects them all to get along.

Polygamy has been proven to be an unsuccessful cultural practice, as studies have shown that where men are permitted to have multiple wives, competition between them increases insecurity and causes greater levels of crime, violence, poverty and gender inequality than in societies that practice monogamous marriage. In the same way, hastily assembling boards and unproven teams is very bad for business. It will cause tensions, squabbles and power grabs, factions and rivalries, all of which detract from the primary purpose of any business: satisfying the customer profitably.

There are many different structures that can be set up at the beginning of new a business, from joint venture to affiliate and supplier partnerships. Use these vehicles to test and refine an approach to a full business partnership.

4. **Agree on your vision.** It's a good idea to go away for at least one uninterrupted weekend to talk all the following through. Since everything is created twice, first in imagination and then in reality, it's critical that potential business partners agree on their vision rather than making it up as they go along. Many partnerships fail because insufficient effort has been put into this. Ask yourself questions like: what is your "reason why"? What are your goals and primary skillset? What value is your business going to create for your customers, and how will you know it's being achieved? Who is your competition and why do you think you can do it better than them? Will you grow organically or through investment or acquisition? And if so, how? Document the answers and put them into a simple business plan.

The question many founders should ask themselves but so often don't is: do you want to own (for example) 80% of a £10 million company, 30% of a £100 million company, or 10% of a £1 billion company? Put another way, do you want an £8 million sale in five years, a £30 million sale in ten, or a £100 million in eleven to twenty years? Scaling the numbers up or down, of course, depending on your business model and sector.

Decide who's going to be responsible for each area of the business and how you are going to fill any gaps. What are your existing commitments in business as well as life, and how might they impact on your performance and ability to deliver? Are you a 24/7 fast-track type? Or do you believe evenings and weekends are sacrosanct? What are your expectations regarding communications, availability and presence for one another?

In most successful business partnerships, there's usually one leader or guardian of the vision and one whose strength is execution. Both roles are equally as critical, so shares are often split 50/50. However, there will be times when both partners disagree on something. Will you have a go-to mentor, non-exec or chairman to help you resolve these, or will one of you have the default "casting vote"? And if so, who?

5. **Don't be fluffy around money.** We're all in business to make money, and this topic needs to be on the agenda right from the start. Is the value each of you creates considered equal by both of you, and if not, how will that be reflected in share allocations? Too many founders agree to split their equity 50-50, but then find themselves doing more than their share of the work while their partner coasts along enjoying life and spending the money they're making. This common situation causes huge resentment, so you need to address the possibility of this upfront. How might this situation show up, and what would it look like if it did? Looking at what could go wrong and putting measures in place to address it mitigates risk.

Always make sure you have an agreement concerning the financial contribution each of you will make to the business. If money or seed capital is involved, terms have to be very clear as to when and how your funds are returned. If you take on others as you grow, do you plan to dilute your shares, or will you put incentives and bonuses in place instead? Are you going to have business or personal mentors and undertake training and development? Will the business pay for all of your travel, entertainment and accommodation, or will you subsidise them personally in the start-up phase? Will your employees have access to training and development, and will the business pay for this? What marketing costs do you consider to be reasonable to begin with, and for what activities should they be used?

You don't need to make these discussions complicated, but recording them and referring back to them when you create your full operations agreement is a great place to start.

The final ingredient of a successful business partnership is the value you're willing to bring to another. If you're someone who seeks to get more than you give, if you have a scarcity mindset, and if you bring anger, impatience and irritation to others, you are not going to be a great business partner for anyone. Work on becoming the very best version of yourself and you'll attract and retain a wonderful business partner who is on their way to becoming the best version of themselves too.

CHAPTER TWENTY:
Your Personal Brand

"Your brand is what other people say about you when you're not in the room." Jeff Bezos, Founder and Chief Executive Officer of Amazon.com

"In the beginning, it was just about the business, now it's about the brand." Richard Branson.

While large multinational companies project their values through their corporate brand, smaller businesses and solopreneurs often build their brand through one or more of their key people. With the power of social media and 35 billion Google searches happening daily, having a great personal brand can truly transform your business success. Your personal brand can be summarised as the consistent experience your customers have of you. It is also about packaging you up in the most attractive way so that your customers will value you more highly and choose you over your competition. These days, many people think anyone who's in business and ignoring the power of personal brand either lives in the age of dinosaurs or has something to hide. So in this chapter, I'm going to give you a four-step system to build the brand of you with integrity.

The value of brand

But before we get into this, and just to remind you how valuable brands can be, I'd like to use the example of Coca Cola. Almost every adult on the planet recognises the distinctive red and white Coca Cola brand logo. Despite being an unhealthy, additive-packed, and not particularly tasty drink, Coca Cola hits one of the top spots on the Interbrand Best Global Brands ranking each year with an estimated brand value of $73.1 billion. There's a real science behind calculating this, by the way, so it's not just a made-up figure. Apple, which encourages us to "Think Different" is also one of the most powerful brands in the world. Its distinctive logo inspires 100% brand recognition in surveys and unparalleled customer loyalty. Apple tops Forbes' annual study of the most valuable brands in the world and is estimated to be worth $170 billion. Its brand value climbs by 10% over last year and represents 21% of the company's recent market value of $806 billion.

Powerful people brands

Let's look at a parallel example of a person who has a powerful personal brand. Richard Branson's playful and fun personal brand has generated massive success for his 200-plus companies, each one of which has benefited hugely from their association with him. He has an incredible ten million followers on LinkedIn, more than anyone else in the world. On Instagram, he describes himself as a "Tie-loathing adventurer and thrill seeker, who believes in turning adventures into reality ... Dr. Yes." He posts happy, smiley pictures of his adventures, friends and loved ones mixed in with inspiring and motivational quotes about leadership and life. He makes everyone feel like they can belong to his club of positive, empowered entrepreneurs for whom life holds no limits. By creating no-holds-barred access to his personal life, he's the living embodiment of a powerfully abundant mindset.

The queen of personal development, Oprah Winfrey, is another example of someone with an incredible personal brand. In fact, like Richard Branson, she's one of the few people in the world who most people recognise just by the mention of her name. Her brand is synonymous with overcoming personal challenge and reaching potential. What sets Oprah apart is her empathy, tone of voice and storytelling abilities. This is the cornerstone of her personal brand, and it's consistent through her speech, body language and the tone of her voice. For example, her Supersoul podcast on iTunes invites you to "awaken, discover and connect to the deeper meaning of the world around you." It "lights up, guides you through life's big questions and helps bring you one step closer to your best self."

Your four-step personal brand system

I know we can't all be Richard Branson or Oprah Winfrey, or have their marketing agencies or brand experts at our disposal, but they've been generous enough to raise the bar and let us follow their lead. So, using their principles, here's your four-step plan to building your successful personal brand. Step one is positioning. Positioning is a concept at the heart of brand marketing and involves creating an overarching headline that differentiates you from your competition. It is very important that this resonates with your authentic personality and way of doing things. My positioning statement, which you'll see on my Instagram feed, is "Loving life, having fun, creating value through connection," as this summarises my attitude to life and my offer in both my property and consulting businesses. Am I always loving life? Am I having fun 24/7? No, like everyone else, day-to-day life has its highs and lows, but it doesn't matter. Positioning expresses powerful intent. This is how you show up in business as well as life.

Step two is brand strategy. This is where you define and crystallise your offer. What value are you bringing to your clients? What do you want them to associate with your name? Is there a subject in which you want to be perceived as an expert? Or are there more general qualities that you want linked to your brand? As an example, here is my own brand strategy statement: "I'm a property and business consultant and high-level connector. I'm also a thought leader and creative producer, offering daily inspiration and value to SME entrepreneurs. I make property and business enjoyable, forgiving and fun."

Step three is brand expression. Think of this as the tone or filter you put on your communications. So think about your visual style, logos and tone of voice, as well as your positioning and ratios as expressed in step one. Think about where you sit on the spectrum of words such as safe, innovative, creative and so on. It's important to revisit this frequently and keep both your profile and brand communications up to date as your business evolves. If you're focussing more on your personal as opposed to corporate brand, remember you should guard against being perceived as narcissistic. So whatever posts you put out, think about the value you're creating for your target audience. What is the take away that will either help, inspire or entertain them?

Step four is your brand system. Where, when, how often, and in what form do you show up? For example, I made a decision earlier this year to build high-level credibility by creating events where I was either speaking or hosting. Other decisions I made were to spend 45 minutes a day on social media and to put out my YouTube videos twice a week. Systems need to be properly implemented, so if you can't do everything yourself, as with everything in your business, engage the power of leverage and get others to do it for you. Internet marketing and associated technologies are advancing all the time, and if you are your own brand creator, you should not get too hung up with trying to understand all the different platforms and channels that you can distribute your brand and content through. I believe it is always best to do what you do well (building your personal brand and associated offer) and leverage the skills, talents and proven systems of others to deliver this on your behalf. Have confidence in your team and let them guide you.

So to have a successful brand, follow my four-step system. Step one, create a powerful and honest positioning statement about yourself. Step two, define your brand strategy and unique offer in an easily understood and communicable form. Step three, decide your brand expression. Think of this as tonality; how business-focussed or warm and personal do you want to be? And how are your posts, videos and blogs going to create value for others? Step four, create your brand system. Decide on the habits you are going to adopt to ensure consistency across multiple platforms, offline as well as online, and brand success will be yours.

CHAPTER TWENTY-ONE:
Reciprocity

Have you ever felt the urge to return a favour for someone who has done something for you before? This is known as the law of reciprocity, and it's one of the key ways we all persuade or influence others.

The law of reciprocity is an instinctive and universally recognised social convention to do with our perceived need to return generous or helpful acts in kind. This convention also says we expect others to return the favours we've done for them. Reciprocity has been around for as long as we humans have been alive. It evolved to improve our chances of survival, as well as our strength in social groups and communities. Even animals do things for others so that they'll receive help when it's needed. Think about monkeys picking fleas off each other or the mutual nuzzling that horses do.

In every country across the world, reciprocal and co-operative behaviours help people to connect and achieve things that would have been impossible on their own. In business especially, reciprocity is used by salespeople and marketers to get customers. Using this law, they might offer financial incentives; for example, a free trial or money-back guarantee. They know that if their product doesn't deliver the experience the customer anticipated, they may not want to buy it after the free trial or they may want their money back. But because on one level the customer feels they got something for nothing, most don't act on these instincts, and so the business wins.

Reciprocity creates results

If you're at the forefront of direct sales or customer acquisition, it's your role to highlight the benefits of your product or service and create that all-important revenue for your business. Reciprocity will help you get the attention of your prospective customer, get them to like and trust you, and then persuade them to buy from you. A good way to generate this is through time and money invested. For example, when I was developing business in media, my company would hire a yacht in Cannes twice a year and host lunches and dinners on it. Although it was an expensive exercise, we were able to track the return on investment and found that creating these memorable and special occasions helped us acquire new clients and achieve repeat business from existing ones. Education and training companies offer free taster events for the same reason. They know that once they've got a captive audience, given them value, and pitched them their next-level offer, they'll recoup their set-up costs and make more substantial profits at the back end. This process is called the sales funnel.

Reciprocity is also helpful as a management tool. Obviously, people will be inclined to work harder and make more effort if they feel appreciated. This starts with a generous or kind word or gesture, which makes them feel valued by the person they're working for. Reciprocity can also be generated by creating opportunities for growth and advancement. A structured career path that helps to develop the employee's knowledge and talents will maintain motivation and job satisfaction. As will regular reviews and attention from people they perceive to be higher up and more in-demand. In essence, if you give first, you get. Fail to give and motivation and employee churn increases.

Reciprocity is also the favourite tool of every prolific networker. Connecting people who can make a positive difference to another's life or business builds a bank of goodwill that networkers call on when they need a favour in return. Networking is an incredibly powerful business tool; hence, the saying "your network is your net worth". But it's not enough just to know lots of people. You have to squeeze reciprocal value from networking by creating favours and making your connections count for others as well as yourself.

If you're using the law of reciprocity in a sales process or negotiation, always make sure that every time you give something, you request something in return. And remember, if you don't ask for this, the people you're dealing with will become accustomed to getting something for nothing and will think they can get away without reciprocating at all.

Social and business currency

The law of reciprocity can also be used as a form of social as well as business currency, building goodwill and smoothing interactions between people. In personal life, reciprocity oils the wheels of social and family interaction. Of course, children are notoriously good at taking without feeling the need to give in return, so sometimes parents need to instruct them in this natural law. This can take the form of "I take you to school every day, which uses up my valuable time. So, you need to help me by keeping your room tidy and doing your homework without me having to nag you."

There are two main types of social reciprocity. The first, which we've already discussed, is material or financial. If someone reads, buy them a book or send them an Audible credit. If they enjoy eating out, take them to dinner. If they move houses, surprise them with a bunch of flowers that will brighten up their living room. If they've got a new job, write them a card to say "congratulations". If you're giving them something they value, you're creating a unique experience for them that they'll want to return. If you're the one that's having stuff bought for you, on the other hand, know that it's because the other person wants and expects something from you in return. As long as you understand there's no such thing as a free lunch, enjoy the attention, gifts and the little game or dance that is reciprocity in action.

The second type of reciprocation is verbal. This is when you make people feel good by the things you say. Sincere compliments can go a long way. If you say things like, "You look beautiful tonight. Thank you for making such an effort," or "I really appreciate you making time in your busy schedule to see me," or "I've enjoyed our conversations so much that it's wonderful to be able to meet you in person," you're giving someone a compliment that shows you value their time and efforts. This will make them feel better about themselves, and in turn, they'll be better disposed towards you and more likely to want to make you feel good, too. If it's personal, just make sure your compliment is sincere and not simply a manipulative tactic. If they're well supported and self-aware, the other person will be able to tell the difference.

You can also generate reciprocity by holding back on attention and keeping the focus on the other person. Ask questions and take an interest in their thoughts and needs. This is also a valuable technique in sales as it will make you appear more interested in someone else's viewpoint, which will then make them relax and trust you. Of course, not everyone will recognise the value you are offering them through this behaviour. But the point is to give it anyway and then see what comes back. Remember, you should always monitor someone's actions more than their words. Actions rarely lie, and they reveal the true regard others have for you. If you're in a committed relationship where you provide value and it's not coming back in kind, tell the other person where they're going wrong and give them a chance to redress the balance. Most people will get lazy and stop making the effort if they're not challenged enough. It's human nature.

Intention not manipulation

Some people feel very uncomfortable with the law of reciprocity because they equate it with manipulation and insincerity. Here, it is the underlying intention and emotional sophistication of both sides that makes the difference. Of course, reciprocity can be deeply manipulative, and it's important to remember this. Ask yourself—is someone doing something good for you because they want you to ignore something else they are doing that hurts you? Or are they doing something that makes you or others suspect they're out to exploit or manipulate you? We humans are so much better than we think at tuning into non-verbal signals that give us the information we need. Listen to your instincts, and if someone makes you uncomfortable or upset, recognise that somewhere along the way, the positive and healthy version of reciprocity has left the room. In this instance, and as always, honesty is the best policy. You, as well as others, can do reciprocity with total integrity, just as you can do it as a manipulative tactic. I'm sure you know which way is best, so put your principles first, then experiment and enjoy.

CONCLUSION

Congratulations! You've started your journey as a Smart Connector – the architect of your amazing business, and life.

I'm so grateful to you for purchasing my book, and reading it to the very end. I hope to have created massive value for you, as this was certainly my intention. If you've enjoyed reading it, I'd love you to leave a review on Amazon. If you want to get to know me personally, or enquire about my online courses, mastermind groups, 1:1 or business partner work, and of course, my (planned for) fabulous retreats in beautiful settings, feel free to email me on jane@janebayler.com. Being an entrepreneur can be a lot of fun, but it's also lonely at times. If you join one of my entrepreneurial success groups, you'll build a powerful network of like-minded people and never be alone on your journey again.

Wishing you all the very best with your relationships in business and life.

Stay connected always.

Jane Bayler

ABOUT THE AUTHOR

Jane Bayler spent most of her career in media and advertising in London, running high level accounts and developing business for companies such as global advertising group Young and Rubicam, and U.S. communications group Interpublic.

She was also M.D. of an international design company, and grew the business to sale and exit, which enabled her to take time off to raise her three girls when they were small.

Having created her first property project, a 'partially subterranean' extension and full refurbishment of a Grade 2 listed building in Buckinghamshire, U.K., she then went on to found a property investment and development company, where she worked with investors and helped them profit from property too.

The Smart Connector draws on Jane's decades of experience with high level business relationships. It is underpinned by her absolute passion and conviction that for sustained business success, people need to come first, always.

Thank you for reading my book. If you enjoyed it, won't you please take a moment to leave me a review at your favourite retailer?

Thanks!

Jane Bayler

Follow me on Twitter:
https://twitter.com/JaneBayler

Friend me on Facebook: https://www.facebook.com/TheSmartConnector

LinkedIn:
https://www.linkedin.com/in/janebayler (personal),
https://www.linkedin.com/company/11864234 (company)

YouTube: https://www.youtube.com/channel/UC2hMlU_NoPn3AvIknPF_JwA

Printed in Great
Britain
by Amazon

31437549R00079